EVE WAS FRAMED

EVE WAS FRAMED

Thoughtful Contributions by Sister

KasiaBartczak[1]

REV. CANDICE CIRESI, ESQ.

A DIVISION OF DEEP RIVER BOOKS

---

[1] Not really a "Sister," more like a second cousin, twice removed.

© 2013 by Rev. Candice Ciresi, Esq. All rights reserved.
2nd Printing 2014.

Trusted Books is an imprint of Deep River Books. The views expressed or implied in this work are those of the author. To learn more about Deep River Books, go online to www.DeepRiverBooks.com.

No part of this publication may be reproduced, stored in a retrieval system, or transmitted in any way by any means—electronic, mechanical, photocopy, recording, or otherwise—without the prior permission of the publisher, except as provided by USA copyright law.

Unless otherwise noted, all Scriptures are taken from the *Holy Bible, New International Version®, NIV®*. Copyright © 1973, 1978, 1984, 2011 by Biblica, Inc.™ Used by permission of Zondervan. All rights reserved worldwide. www.zondervan.com

Translation adaptations from *The Almighty, Circa 1400 BC/BCE*

ISBN 13: 978-1-63269-172-9
Library of Congress Catalog Card Number: 2013901278

Contents

Act 1: Genesis 1, Creation in General 1
Act 2: Genesis 2, The Creation, More Specifically 35
Act 3: Genesis 3, The Fall 53
Act 4: Genesis 4, Cain and Abel 79
Act 5: Genesis 5, Adam to Noah 103
Act 6: The Tree of Life 105

    Sabbatone 115
    Annual Festivities 117
    Passover—Death of the Lamb 118
    Firstfruits of the Barley Harvest—Resurrection 131
    Shavuot/Pentecost—Betrothal. 136
    Rosh Hashanah—Start of Judgment Day. 142
    Yom Kippur—Sentencing. 146
    Sukkot—Messiah's Birthday. 149
    Kingdom of G. 158
    Getting to the Tree of Life. 163

Act 7: Story Sabbath. 167

Act 1: Genesis 1, Creation in General

I wasn't entirely sure how to respond when Gabriel asked me if I wanted to see the big show that night. Whenever heaven holds a big event, it is always worth exploring. Of course, when Gabriel brings the news, it is only that much more important. He has a knack for communication. After all, his gift of speech earned him the role of heavenly public relations consultant: when Gabriel spoke, angels listened. That's partly because he didn't bother delivering dull news or otherwise routine events, but also because you really can't help but listen. Gabriel has the smoothest voice with such a calming effect. It's the gentle, sultry sound you expect to hear from Barry White doing yoga. Even his reading of the fine print on a refrigerator warranty gives you a slight thrill, joined with a sedating comfort.

I showed up late to the event to find legions upon legions of angels gathered in varying levels and planes surrounding the heavenly throne, all eyes focused on a distant void. I think that is my gift, really. Not the ability to focus on voids, but the knack to never be on time regardless of how much I prepare. You would think that as an angel I could defy time and space—angels are not subject to either—yet for some inexplicable reason, I still find myself popping up after the fact. Michael frequently teases that when G calls me to come forth, I'll be fifth. Great—Gabriel gets the smooth voice, and I get tardiness. Good thing I live in eternity—no one should ever notice!

Of course, my inability to be on time blurs any ability to tell a story in chronological order; but that doesn't stop me. I have heard many, many humans who not only miss the timing of a story but the point as well. Hopefully, I can be accused of only one of these errors. If you can simply suspend your concept of time, my story makes perfect sense. Not many people understand the nature of time, or even that of heaven and earth. I laugh when I hear about history classes that go back just a few hundred or thousand years. That's not even a day in my time.

The other thing people don't understand is creation. And quantum physics. And taxes. Of course, even angels don't get those. Except for fallen ones. They created them, after all.

But I digress.

"It is so dark over there. I can't see a thing. Has anybody seen Uriel? Maybe he could shed some light on the situation." I chuckle at my own remark. Uriel is known for always having something on fire nearby. He is the pyromaniac of the angels. Once humans really got moving outside the garden, Uriel spent a great deal of time frequenting barbecues. Still does. He likes to disguise himself as a short, stocky, balding man who wears black socks with sandals.

Oh, wait—the creation! I remember the creation, or is it *remembered*? There's that time thing again. Do you recall something in the past in the past tense? I don't get it. The beautiful thing about being an angel is we never have to conjugate our verbs. Everything is. It is now. Even the stuff that was, is.

That is why I can tell you in the present tense about an event that happened thousands of years ago and is recorded in a well-known book called Genesis that you have probably read and could read a dozen times. The only reason I am giving a play-by-play is because, oftentimes, people scan over the "In the Beginning" as casually as they read "Once Upon a Time." But Genesis isn't fiction, nor is it to be read so casually. In fact, each verse is so poignant, potent, and prophetic that people are slighted when they think the book is solely about a woman setting up a man for an illicit apple-eating contest. There is so much more to the story; hopefully, like Uriel, I can shed some light on the first few chapters of the book of Genesis. Contrary to some beliefs, it isn't about Adam taking a fall for a woman. The story isn't about woman being some seductive temptress luring the man away from G. If you are of the opinion that woman singlehandedly brought about the Fall, I have three words for you: Eve was framed.

Anyway, the big show is starting, started.

In the beginning G created the heavens and the earth.

This isn't just a catchy line to start an intriguing story; although, it is quite catchy.[2] Every sentence of Scripture conveys something more, something more profound, something to make you say "Ah!" That's why I am here. I want to help you notice the significance of the verses. Think of me as an ethereal tour guide like Sacagawea to Lewis and Clark, Beatrice to Dantes or Dory to Marlin.[3]

See, the first thing G gave was time—"the beginning." Before this moment, G was—or is. Anyway, G didn't worry about watches, clocks, or calendars. You might think that being outside of time would be mind-numbingly boring. Eternity is hard to fathom, especially if you watch a clock; but the illusion of time can be sensed by humans on some level. After all, time is a relative illusion.[4] Einstein explains relativity by saying that an hour with a beautiful woman seems like a second, and a second on a red-hot cinder seems like an hour. Albert really will get—er, *got* that right.

Well, G's presence is like sitting with a beautiful person, but without having to end the conversation because of a meeting or the closing of the day. Many humans suspect angels simply pounce around the clouds wearing togas and playing harps. The only people who really do that are people who join us right out of college … and Socrates. The rest understand G's reference to such was merely

---

[2] You can almost envision the words scrolling upwards against a backdrop of space.

[3] Nemo's dad.

[4] Time with relatives often appears significantly longer than with other people.

metaphorical. Raphael—the artist, not the archangel or the ninja turtle—painted a picture of chubby little cherubs looking bored in the heavenly abode. We don't have time to be bored because, frankly, we don't have time.

There was an old joke about three men who all learned they were going to die in two weeks. The first man stated he would spend his remaining time at a beach in the Caribbean. The second man said he was going to spend his remaining time in the mountains. The third man announced he was going to go stay with his mother-in-law.

"Your mother-in-law?" the first two questioned. "Why?"

The third man replied, "It'll be the longest two weeks of my life."

For angels, everything happens at once—in seconds. It goes by so quickly, I can't keep time straight. Time only means something to the finite and the mortal. When humans behave with the illusion that they are immortal in their current form, they have so little respect or appreciation for the time they have. For angels, it doesn't matter much either, but because we are immortal, as is. If humans truly appreciated the brevity of their time on earth, they wouldn't squander it so easily. It really isn't that difficult a concept. Time is the T-shirt placed on the infant soul. As the soul grows and evolves, it moves through and into the time covering, until such a day comes that it has outgrown the shirt. The soul doesn't go away; it just goes naked.

Of course, it is easier to explain the time thing when you simply reflect on where you are in your life now.

It is always the *now* that matters. Your past has very little to do with your future. If you were in Chicago and wanted to go to Beaufort, South Carolina, the one question that will prove most useless is, "Well, where were you before Chicago?" The critical questions for life, as for any destination, are: "Where are you going?" and "How are you getting there?" That's why you can't remember every detail of your past; it just isn't as important as where you are striving to go. The critical choices are forward-looking, not backward-looking. This doesn't mean you shouldn't reflect on the past; it just means you should be careful on what memories you choose to reflect. If the memories you savor propel you to improve yourself, others, or the world—then, embrace them. If they cause you to languish, judge, or fall into despair, then you must simply choose to either think on better things or create the positive memories that can move you forward. The ability to select and hold on to whatever memories you want is an amazing and often underappreciated gift that humans were given.[5]

You humans gather all those memories of your life that led up to this exact moment in time and pack them in a mental suitcase. It begins as a small carry-on but quickly grows into the checked luggage that you simply label "The Past." You decide what events from your Past to cram in the corners in hopes that no one will ever see them; yet, you just can't seem to let them go. You decide which memories from your Past to fling around so everyone can see. Surprisingly enough, the memories you carry around and hold on to in your suitcase of life show the world less about where you have been and more about where you are going.

If you are unsure where you are going in life you may carry a great deal of baggage. After all, you don't know who you are going to have to impress or where you will end up. Pull out the memories that allow you to justify to the world why you are in the state you are in. Belabor the memories that give you the desperate justifications for why you are not living up to other human's expectations or have otherwise surpassed them. Pull out the memories that show why you simply must be loved. Pull out the memories to prove that you are smart, strong, a victim, whatever other label you may have assigned yourself. But, ultimately, human suitcases should be empty.

You see, this is why G made you naked. You don't have to put on pretense. There is no image, no ideal, and no baggage. You don't need a suitcase if you are comfortable with the suit you are wearing. You also don't need a suitcase if you know, *know*, just *know* that you have everything you need waiting for you at your intended destination.

Most humans are not comfortable naked. They can get hung up on the sad or angry. But negative feelings should pass right through you. If the bad thoughts are pooling inside, you need to flush and clean them out. If you let them build up too much, you'll clog your

---

[5] Goldfish, not so much.

system. Test everything; hold on to the good.[6] Holding on to the bad just makes your hands stinky.

Ultimately, your mind is the one thing that you will carry with you wherever you go. Given this fact, you would think that humans would be a bit more careful about what they put into their brains and what they allow to languish there. If you want good to be with you always, put good into your mind.

There *is* good. G said so many times. Yet some humans can't always seem to find it in the present. For instance, here you are, in the now. You can pick anything you want on which to focus your brain. You can look around, smell, see, touch, hear, yell, laugh—whatever. You can fill your thoughts with absolutely anything. This is the primary distinguishing factor between humans and most angels. Humans often actually *pick* something bad, scary, or sad to think about. This completely baffles me about humans. They will *choose* to reflect or anticipate the scary or painful, thereby making the *now* completely empty. They choose the bad thoughts and feel regret, shame, or insecurity. Conversely, they look forward to events that have never transpired and come up with crazy possibilities and worst-case scenarios. The beauty of the present becomes stripped of its wonder and awe with the regrets of the past and fears of the future.

Most of the time, the present is simple. It is without fanfare and trumpet blasts. It is often the common routine of brushing teeth, washing dishes, working, taking a bath.[7] The present, a majority of the time, seems dull. This tends to frustrate some people. But it is the ordinary and everyday life that begins to define you. Those things you do every day are the things you will excel at doing. Think of an athlete or painter. He or she didn't just pick up the sport or the paintbrush and excel all of a sudden. The Olympic swimmer swam, *every* day. He didn't pick a different activity every day and then decide on swimming the day before the competition. The painter

---

[6] I can't take credit for that line. Paul will say it in his letter to Timothy, but he isn't created yet, chronologically.

[7] Hopefully.

painted a lot. The Super Bowl champion practiced and practiced and practiced—football, not knitting.[8]

So what you do with your every day and ordinary time defines and creates your extraordinary skill. If you complain all the time, you will become a good complainer. If you whine all the time, you become a great whiner. If you pick out flaws in people, you will become judgmental. But if you start showing love, reading, studying the Word of G, those ordinary, small things will create an extraordinary *you* and will change the world as well.

While many people possess remarkable talents, it is the honing of the talent through repetition that transforms the ordinary into the extraordinary. Whether you know it or not, ordinary and silence can create extraordinary and explosive big bangs that fill the formless and empty voids.

You are deceived if you believe the ordinary is dull! The newer, better, faster, cooler only make you feel older, worse, slower, geeky. If you are training yourself always to seek the bigger and better, you will not be happy with smaller and average. If you train yourself into believing there needs to be more, then you will begin to perform small tasks to satisfy that hunger. You get so good at those little tasks, intended to propel you to the new and better, that you begin to master them ... and they begin to master you. It is Attention Deficit Disorder of the Spirit (ADDS), where thoughts of *It is not enough* replay and repeat throughout your mind so much that you are always looking for something else. Humans go running through the kingdom of G so fast, bent on satisfying their preset expectations, only to miss all the glory and beauty adorning the halls. At some point in time, humans will lose the ability to be, to listen, and to reflect. Their minds will receive so much external stimulation; they become internally numb or just empty. They can't hear that still, small voice within because they are too focused on the with-*out*.

You can't hear the voice of G if you aren't still enough to listen. G doesn't speak with the thundering voice of a cartoon superhero. G whispers. To hear the voice of G, one only needs to quiet the soul.

---

[8] Not to say there haven't been some football players who knitted in some spare time.

It's a hard skill to master as it involves letting go of those worldly concerns that pop in and out of your mind with all the subtlety of whack-a-mole moles. But, by continually ignoring the worldly moles, your skills improve and you become better able to focus on the divine. Inner peace comes not from good mole whacking but from unplugging the worldly machine, letting go of the noisy, meaningless interruptions for enough time to focus on what really matters.

Even if you cannot find a way to unplug the machine, G can create a power surge that will ensure well-directed thoughts. G indicates that whatever is true, noble, right, pure, lovely, admirable, excellent, or praiseworthy, you should think on those things to find peace.[9] The greatest point of this directive is that humans *can* choose. In fact, G encourages good choices. Whenever you humans start falling prey to bad thoughts, remember this directive. Humans will be given dominion over the earth in the creation process, but even more important is that all humans have complete dominion over their minds. You always, always have the power to choose your thoughts—and to choose to give that power away.

Ah, ever since that incident in the garden, many humans have felt compelled to ensure that something negative taints their mood and to believe that what they have or who they are is not good enough. They eat from the Tree of the Knowledge of Good and Evil every single day. People shake their fists and curse Adam and Eve for eating the forbidden fruit, yet when they have the option themselves of choosing good or bad, they will still think of the bad or even act on the bad. Humans have always known the good, yet they keep introducing themselves to the bad.

Oh, the garden! There goes my chronology again. The creation is occurring! Where are my manners?

> Now the earth was formless and empty, darkness was over the surface of the deep, and the Spirit of G was hovering over the waters.

---

[9] Check Philippians 4 for more information. Or check out four Philippians, if you can find any.

So G began with time and a whole lot of nothing.

And G said, "Let there be light," and there was light.

There was still nothing to look at, but now you could see it a whole lot better. Now the earth was a *well-lit,* formless, and empty void. Like a craftsman walking into his shop with a large project in mind, G turned on the light and inspected what G had to work on and the logical steps required for getting there.[10] It is important to realize that G doesn't work quickly or without a plan.[11] G doesn't operate under some forced deadline. Being G and all, there isn't a supervisor to give ratings or performance reviews, so there is a blessed ability to skip all the bureaucracy and red tape generally required when introducing a new product into the market.

You know this is heaven—no policies, no bureaucracy, no FDA approvals, and no need for lawyers.[12] There is deliberate thought. It is a slow, patient, precise process—although the creation of the platypus does seem to contravene the fact that there was conscious thought given to the crazy design of the creature.

Speaking of thought and creation, scientists all seem to agree that the universe is expanding. So if we were to hit the rewind button in order to get a glimpse of the beginning of the universe—outside of the insight I am giving you now—the universe would retract until it was reduced to a point of singularity. The prevalent belief will come to be that something dramatic and impressive occurred at this point of singularity—generally summed up as the Big Bang theory.[13] Regardless of what humans will come to believe relating to evolution, creation, or some combination thereof, what cannot be disputed is that there was a point in time where *something* came

---

[10] Unlike me. I would have tried to cram tab A into slot K, with five nuts and two screws remaining.

[11] In fact, many will come to realize that the first five books of the Bible operate as a blue print for creation.

[12] Heaven has often been called paradise due to the notable lack of attorneys and performance reviews.

[13] Not to be confused with a popular television show.

from *nothing*. That fact can never be disproved or explained by science.

I am baffled as to why science would want to take the Creator out of the creation. To take the hand of G out of creation diminishes human life to nothing more than an accident. It further would support that humans are not equal, because there is no worth assigned to any particular life aside from luck. In fact, evolution, in and of itself, argues that only the strong survive; in nature, some animals allegedly are superior and survive because they adapt better. If humans default to a purely naturalistic viewpoint, then the survival of the fittest theory should carry over to humans. Absent a Creator, there would not be equality among humans. The weaker of the human species—the children, the elderly, the sick, the disabled—could all be overthrown in the name of nature. In support of this belief there will be philosophers who will come to argue that equality is a lie, that there simply are those who are smarter and better and should prevail because of these points.[14] They present that from a purely naturalistic perspective, only the strong survive.

But through creation, every person will have been a child, most will know sickness at some point in their lives, and many will be elderly. As every human will have been the weaker of society at some point in his or her life, the reaction should be compassion, not superiority. Nature, absent G, weans the weak through defeat. Nature, with G, builds up the weak thereby making everyone stronger.

There is no ranking of people, no categories of privilege, no caste system with G. There cannot be. The Creator heralds that every human life is sacred. It is the Creator who asks that you honor and love every other person as much as yourself, no exceptions. It is the Creator who bestows equality. Because each life is sacred and loved, each human *has* value and *should* value each human.

But I still hear the argument that "If there is a Creator, why doesn't the Creator just flat out prove its existence?"

I am going to flip this question on you. What if I were to say that I don't believe that your mother exists or ever existed. Now what?

---

[14] Friedrich Nietzsche posited that belief. By the way, Nietzsche is dead.

You would probably say "Well, I'm here, aren't I? She has to exist because my existence is proof that she exists!" I may come back and tell you that I don't believe that people are created from parents. I believe people are the result of scientific experiments, a massive explosion, or genetic mutation. I don't believe you were created, therefore there is no creator."

You could then come back and produce a birth certificate. You could show me a signed, stamped, and very official document recording the birth of your mother. You point to the doctor's signature. You can show me a witness' signature. You can show me dates and times. I would tell you that I don't know that doctor. How do I know he was telling the truth? You would argue that the writing was made by people of integrity who witnessed the events and was verified by others. I don't believe the written word.

You could tell me that I could read about your mom and her amazing accomplishments in dozens of different books. I argue its fiction.

You could tell me that I could speak to other people about the wonderful things your mom has done for them and how she changed their lives. I don't believe them; they're delusional.

You could tell me that I could come and visit her. You would give me directions to the house. I can drive, walk, bike, or run to meet this woman. Frankly, I don't want to do all that work. I want you to convince me she exists, but I am not going to put any effort into meeting her myself.

Exhausted by my arguments, you finally throw up your hands and shout, "Just because you don't believe or won't try to meet her doesn't mean she doesn't exist. I have seen her. I have felt her. I have loved her; and she loves me!" To which, I could only say … "Amen."

> G saw that the light was good, and G separated the light from the darkness.

So then it was dark again, then light, then dark—a bit like a child who just discovered a light switch and the effect it has on the room. It's on again; it's off again. We all enjoyed the light show, a bit funky.

It could have used a disco ball, but who am I to second-guess the Creator?

I should take a moment to address a quick point. This "quick point" is the meaning of "good". This word is going to pop up quite a bit and I should, at least, provide you with a baseline definition before I began throwing it at you. Good is *that which draws close to G*. I will actually touch on it more, later, but this little appetizer should hold you over until we present the larger course.

G called the light "day," and the darkness G called "night."

G could have very well called them *on* and *off*.

And there was evening, and there was morning—the first day.

There G went again, setting up the time thing. There are the general beginning and end, and now this strand is broken up into even increments called days. So efficient. I like how G did the day thing. It starts off dark and slowly moves to a bright morning and a sunny afternoon. I think this is G's way of showing people how their lives should move—from the dark unknown into a beautiful sunrise and then a pure light. The new day begins in darkness, just like a chalkboard. You draw, you write, you try new things until the board is completely covered with ideas, pictures, and lots of mistakes. The day changes, the board is clean. *Making* a mistake is not bad; *repeating* the same mistake is not good. Eventually, you learn to stop making certain mistakes. Well, you *should* learn anyway. It's like getting a clean slate every day. The artwork on the chalkboard gradually improves as long as you are willing to learn. There is a famous poem that will be written by an elementary school teacher named Kathleen Wheeler entitled "A New Leaf" that conveys this thought almost as well as Gabriel could read it, but as we have limited legal representation in Heaven, I lack the intricacies of copyright law so will simply direct you to explore the poem on your own.

Many times people seem to carry over baggage throughout the days—missing the entire point of the demarcation of time. People become so focused on a problem—an event, a feeling—that they completely miss the new slate, the new opportunities, the rebirth. They lose the now … er, or lost the now. These time breaks give you a great opportunity to, well, to change. People mess up; that is a fundamental trait of humanness.

Time was a gift G gave to humans that is grossly undervalued. Imagine never sleeping. Imagine never having any downtime. You just evolve—like those pesky houseflies that are born and move from larvae to death in a day. I don't even know if flies sleep. I should know that, being an angel and all, but then again, I'm not omniscient, so I don't feel too bad about fly ignorance. Anyway, imagine going from birth to toddler, teenager, adult, and death with no pause or breaks. It is already hard enough for people to make good use of their time, but if they never slept, work hours would be crazy. There could never be enough coffee breaks. Humans would always be on the go. The beautiful thing about sleeping is that it forces you to simply be still. It's a forced break in the action that actually allows you to be a human *being* as opposed to a human *doing*. G could have kept life as one long moment, but breaking it up into increments reminds people that they have a chance to start all over. Each day is a new chalkboard.

> "Let there be an expanse between the waters to separate water from water." So G made the expanse and separated the water under the expanse from the water above it. G called the expanse "sky."

It looked like a modern-day school project where oil and water are poured into a jar and then shaken real hard. Imagine that. The sky and water just got to separating, although there wasn't any shaking. That would have been funny.

And then off came, then on—the second day.

> "Let the water under the sky be gathered to one place, and let dry ground appear." And it was so. G called the dry ground "land," and the gathered waters G called "seas."

This is truly a remarkable day for most humans, as it resulted in the creation of beaches and subsequently, the drinks with the little umbrellas in them. G saw that this distinction was good; therefore, we angels knew it was good. This is the thing that angels know; we know good. We know, because we are manifestations of the attributes of G—kind of like fingers on a very complex hand, each finger unique in size, shape, and function, yet truly part of a larger being. We have the understanding and the will to do good because our larger being is good. Of course, there is always that unruly finger that keeps gravitating toward the nose.

And G saw that it was good.

You might notice that the second day noticeably lacks an "... it was good" comment from G. This isn't because it was bad but simply that what was started on the second day wasn't complete until the third. This is why you will see the "... it is good" comment twice on the third day.

> "Let the land produce vegetation: seed-bearing plants and trees on the land that bear fruit with seed in it, according to their various kinds." And it was so. The land produced vegetation: plants bearing seed according to their kinds and trees bearing fruit with seed in it according to their kinds.

I tried to encourage G to refrain from including Brussels sprouts in the creation process but was calmly assured that someone out there likes them.

And G saw that it was good.

Even the Brussels sprouts. Weird.

There is an interesting trend in the way G created: nothing could have been done out of order. G could not have made plants before land, else they would have just sat there, untouched ... much like those Brussels sprouts. The water was there before the fish. The plants and grass were there before the animals. The deliberate thought and careful planning ensured that nothing was without purpose or usefulness; and everything was for the good.[15]

---

15 And arguably ISO compliant.

And there was off, and there was on—the third day.

"Let there be lights in the expanse of the sky to separate the day from the night, and let them serve as signs to mark seasons and days and years, and let there be lights in the expanse of the sky to give light on the earth."

I'm going to ask you to put that bit about the "serve as signs …" on the back burner for a little while. Let it simmer. We will add some more ingredients to that point shortly.

And it was so. G made two great lights—the greater light to govern the day and the lesser light to govern the night. G also made the stars. G set them in the expanse of the sky to give light on the earth, to govern the day and the night, and to separate light from darkness.

G heard my request for a disco ball. Okay. Well, maybe the lights are a bit more than special effects. The Book of Proverbs explains that G's Word is a lamp, or a light, for your path. But the book of 2 Peter[16] provides deeper insight. The Word of G is a "light shining in a dark place *until* the 'morning star rises in your hearts'" (the emphasis on *until* is mine). The Word of G in written form is a light to help humans navigate dark and unfamiliar waters—kind of like an owner's manual for life. It is the light that governs the night. But when the Word takes life through application and love, the greater light of the Messiah, himself, governs. Both lights separate light from darkness. In fact, it is the greater light that causes the lesser light to glow.

And G saw that it was good.

Especially when "Stayin' Alive" was played really loud.

And there was off, and there was on—the fourth day.

---

[16] There have actually been thousands of people with the name Peter. It wasn't the second Peter who wrote the book; it's just the second book attributed to the apostle Peter.

"Let the water teem [Go Teem!] with living creatures, and let birds fly above the earth across the expanse of the sky."

So G created the great creatures of the sea and every living and moving thing with which the water teems [Go Teem!], according to their kinds, and every winged bird according to its kind.

Some humans believe that G also created beer on this day, as it commonly accompanies the fish and fishing.

And G saw that it was good. G blessed them.[17] "Be fruitful and increase in number and fill the water in the seas, and let the birds increase on the earth."

Many people wonder why G would tell animals to be fruitful. Generally, fruit was something reserved for certain plant life. Biologically speaking, fruit is an indicator of the type of specimen with which you are dealing. When you see a tree you don't recognize, looking at the fruit helps to identify the tree. An orange tree and an apple tree may seem similar before they begin to produce fruit, but once the fruit appears, you can distinguish the trees. Of course, if a tree is unhealthy, the fruit starts to wither or show signs of disease. You also can tell the health of the tree by the quality of the fruit. A really sick tree does not produce healthy fruit.

Physically speaking, "fruitful" means being healthy. Now I'm not advocating that you drop the book and join a yoga class because, well, 1, I want you to read the book; and, 2, we are talking about animals right now. So, worst-case scenario, you can drop the book and sign your pet up for yoga classes.[18] While we are currently on the subject of animals being fruitful, it will be expected of humans, as well. Most animals are keen on the need to be physically healthy as failure to oblige in this area generally results in becoming easy prey.

---

[17] The fish, not the beer.

[18] Puts a whole new meaning to "up dog."

Theologically speaking, bearing fruit is correlated with doing good deeds. After all, a plant's fruit doesn't benefit the plant itself; it benefits those who are hungry. People understood this well into—and after—the first century. Somewhere along the line, the understanding gets blurred. A person who is healthy in mind and spirit will bear the fruit of good deeds and good works. Good deeds tell the world you are healthy in mind and body. G expects people to be and to do good. It is not enough in life to simply refrain from doing bad; humans need to take the extra step and do good.

Most major religions recognize the value of loving acts through good deeds. Judaism heralds the Word of G, prayer, and good deeds as the pillars of the faith. Islam recognizes charity as one of its pillars, and Christianity recognizes that "faith without works is dead." There simply must be compassion extended to others without the demand for compensation or personal gain. Like the fruit of a plant, you simply must be benefiting the hungry.

Not only do humans need to bear fruit but they also need pruning. You need to cut out or modify the things, people, and habits that prevent your ability to be fruitful.

A human's pruning is spiritual strength conditioning. It's a workout for the soul. Humans understand the need to push the body in order to get physically stronger; they tend to forget the need to push their spirits to make them strong as well. Humans need to be strong in the face of adversity, calm during the storms and humble during the confrontations. Pruning a human tree involves spiritual weightlifting.

Spiritual weightlifting doesn't come easy. You learn to lift small weights—or trials—without complaining, without anger, and with patience. You challenge yourself by not cracking under the stress when the weight gradually increases. You work out—learning tolerance, compassion, and gratitude—so you can handle the pressure. If or when someone drops a large dumbbell of catastrophe on you, you aren't crushed under its weight but simply exert your strength to lift the burden. In fact, the lightweight problems in life are easily dismissed. You barely notice the small things. At some point, you become strong enough that heavier things don't crush you. You are happier longer because you can handle problems, burdens, and weights without a second thought. Happiness needs no justification; it is evidence of spiritual strength.

G gave animals the fruitful directive first. They seemed to figure it out better than humans. Animals only hurt other animals to eat or avoid being eaten. Of course, at the time they were created there was no need for defensive maneuvering. The healthy, fruitful animals are the least likely to fall prey to a stalking predator. The same concept applies to humans. The spiritually weak are easy prey for people seeking to do harm. Predators attack the weak because they believe they will be successful in the attempt.

Animals also trump humans in that they don't generally plot revenge, get jealous, act judgmental, or feel self-conscious. Cheetahs aren't jealous that tigers have slimming stripes, nor do tigers mock hippos for looking chubby. In fact, the animals are pretty indifferent to how they and the other animals look. You have never heard an animal complain about being naked—wait … yes, I am sure of it—no animal has ever complained about being naked. In fact, the only complaints of which I am aware are when small pets are dressed up in funny little costumes by humans. Animals must be trained and conditioned to lose their fruitfulness. The first time a pod of dolphins swim near a cruise ship and one dolphin yells back, "Dudes, don't jump! We're naked!" you will know they have lost the sense of good.

And there was off, and there was on—the fifth day.

"Let the land produce living creatures according to their kinds: livestock, creatures that creepeth on the ground, and wild animals, each according to its kind." And it was so.

Look! Notice G made the "creatures that creepeth"—G made creeps.

G made the wild animals according to their kinds, the livestock according to their kinds, and all the creatures that creepeth on the ground according to their kinds. And G saw that it was good.

Then G took on a more contemplative nature.[19] Before, G simply spoke as if everything was simply setting the stage for what was to come, and it was so. "Lights! Camera! Fish!" But now something was different. Now the story really begins to get interesting.

> "Let us make man in our image, in our likeness, and let them rule over the fish of the sea and the birds of the air, over the livestock, over all the earth, and over all the creatures that move and creep along the ground."

Let "us" make man in "our" image. People often wonder who or what the "us" is in this sentence. There is the big G, and then there is the Messiah, the Christ—Jesus. Of course, I cannot mention these two names and leave out the Holy Spirit. It is these three attributes, three facets, three beings that comprise G. This is not in any way suggesting polytheism, as there is only One.

In order to explain the Trinity better, I can analogize with a human, any one human ... let's pick a guy named Bob. You can picture Bob in your head. You would argue that Bob is one guy. Now, if Bob were to lose his arm—does he become a new person? What if Bob lost a leg, his eyesight, or his hair? Does the change in Bob warrant a new name and identity? Of course not. The loss of a body part doesn't diminish the person of Bob. In fact, even time will change the Bob of whom you are thinking, as Bob is probably vastly different from what Bob looked like twenty years ago, ten years ago, or even five years ago. Bob will also probably be different in another twenty years, but he will always be Bob. Therefore, there is more to Bob than his physical makeup. But this physical aspect of Bob is what will allow him to feed the poor, visit the sick, and relate in a way that most people can understand. People crave the tangible and need physical comfort. Bob's body can satisfy that need. Although there is a great deal more to Bob than just his body, when Bob dies, that physical makeup will seem like everything. Many people feel they have lost their loved ones at death because of the importance given to the body.

---

[19] Pause here for dramatic effect.

Body aside, there is a character to Bob. He has a personality, feelings, goals, and direction. This character is commonly called a *spirit*, and most people recognize that an individual's spirit outlives the body.

Now, there is also the *mind*. Whereas the character tends to have more personable traits, the mind is the logical mechanism for choice. It is this part of Bob that can effectuate self-discipline, make choices, and direct the character and the spirit. It is the mind that *directs* the body to move, to create, to feed the poor. The body doesn't act on its own will, but on the will of the mind. You would never think to say that Bob is multi-personed, although you should concede that he is multifaceted. It is this way with G.

The primary difference between G and Bob is that there may be times when Bob feels dissonance; his body may want something that his brain knows he should not have. With G, there is no such dissonance. Bob's spirit may encourage action that is discouraged by his bounds of logic. The apostle Paul speaks about not doing what he knows he should do and doing what he knows he should not do.[20] In Paul's case,[21] his spirit and his mind are at odds. With G the three parts are always in harmony.[22]

Of course, there is a simple example of a three-in-one on a human level. Look at the developing fetus. There are three distinct genetic attributes occurring within each and every fetus. One is the genetic contribution of the father. Two is the genetic contribution and the nutrients supplied by the mother. Three is the unique blood and identity of the fetus itself. The fetus is not without unity or connection to the parents. The three are in one in that body. In fact, every human is three in one: a little of a woman, a little of a man, and a lot of a unique identity.

Humans, in the image of G, have three-in-one qualities, but you are similar to G, not identical. *Similar.* Humans often wonder why, if they are made in the image of G, does bad reside in them? That's easy: humans are the *image* of G; they are not G. A camera

---

[20] Not to be confused with Sinatra's do-be-dos or Shaggy's Scooby-do.

[21] And often in Bob's …

[22] Just like an old-fashioned love song coming down in three-part harmony.

can capture your image, but that image will lack the same depth of character you possess.[23]

The early Jewish people believed that humans became more in the image of G when they did loving acts. Still, many humans wondered why G even bothered creating humans. Skeptical people see humans crawling ant like through some divine terrarium while G looks on in amusement. Humans are not G's pets any more than children are their parents' pets. Humans were created out of love, intimacy, and relationship. Of course, there is the one incident with the angels whom many of us believe led G to this development.

See, angels have been with G. We just are. We didn't choose to be, but then again, most of us would never choose otherwise. There is peace, rejoicing, fun, acceptance of all, and an occasional sporting event when we are connected to good. However, there is an angel or two—or a thousand or so—who want to opt out. They believe some are worthy of more acceptance than others. They want to know bad and good, not just good. They are the fingers that want to try their hand at something else. So G creates something that has just that—free will. Ever since the fall of so many angels, we have a lot of vacancies to fill. G isn't going to fill those spots with just anybody. They need to be people who *want* to be here. Of course, just because we hire them to fill the spots doesn't make us the same, but there will be unity in purpose and beliefs. Life on earth is a sort of interview process: "What are your goals in life? Where do you see yourself in five hundred years? Are you a team player?" If you live your life with the belief that there is nothing beyond or better than yourself, you may not be a good fit.

Another consideration for the "us" in this section will be explored when I get to the passage that humans call Genesis 2, but I am trying so hard to maintain chronology here!

> So G created man in G's own image, in the image of G created him; male and female G created them.

---

[23] Depending on who you are, I suppose. If you didn't have any depth to begin with, the image may not be that far off.

There is something very important here—just as there is something important in everything G says. G chooses words purposefully and carefully. Notice how G states that man is created as singular, and then humans—male and female—are created in plural. There are two distinct creations going on here: (1) a singular, and (2) a plural. This is a critical passage on which I will expand later; please put this pot on the back burner with that other pot to simmer for a bit, as it will make sense further on.

G created "them"—humans—"male and female." Why do humans always forget this part? G created both male and female. G points out right now that both male and female are created. The name Adam means "human," or "one formed from the ground." G made them and named them "Human." The word *them* means more than one. In fact, in case you forget the fact that G made multiple people, male and female, G brings it up again a few chapters later during the lineage of Noah. But since Noah isn't created yet, we will have to wait to tell that part. Anyway, the creation of both genders explains a great deal about how the earth managed to populate itself with only two people. There were more than two people.

So the story begins. I remember it like it is now. Numerous people are meandering around the earth, male and female. The earth is a beautiful place, quite conducive to natural living. Good neighborhood, nice views, lots of amenities. It is quite a different picture than the world as you may know it. No one has a belly button.

Imagine G looking into a mirror and G's reflection burned into that mirror. Keep in mind that it is only a reflection, but it is a reflection of something truly great. The mirror falls into millions of pieces, with each shard reflecting a different portion of G. Now, think of a potter who wants to house each of these beautiful, reflective shards in individual vases. The potter took clay from all over the world and made a mosaic of people of differing vases of various shapes, sizes, and colors. No vase is better than any other vase; in fact, the vase is rather irrelevant compared to what it houses. The goal should never be to improve the vase but to discover the potential and beauty of what is inside—inside your vase and the vases of others.

Ah, humans will eventually become more concerned with how their vases look than discovering the images within the vases. Ironic that humans would be drawn to and fixate on the part of their beings with the shortest life span. They know that regardless of how they look on the outside, there is more to them deep inside, something profound and quintessential. However, despite this knowing, they will spend far less time on beautifying the spirit than the body.

Interestingly enough, there will come a time in history when people take actual vases that are broken and use them as lanterns. Obviously, people couldn't run around holding fire in their hands as a source for light. Not for very long anyway. So they sought out broken vases, put the fire within, and let the light shine through! They don't try to beautify the broken lamp. They don't hide the breaks. In fact, it is the brokenness that makes the light shine through and gives the vase its value. In other words, it is not bad to be broken if you use that brokenness for good.

Since I am on the topic of light, I can't help but reflect forward to a time when Jesus will speak of a parable involving ten virgins. The story tells about ten virgins awaiting the bridegroom. All ten virgins have lamps. Five of the virgins brought oil; five did not. The bridegroom, through a delayed flight, traffic, or for whatever reason, arrives late in the evening; in fact, it's dark. The five virgins lacking oil ask those with oil to give up some of their stash. The virgins with oil decline, as they may not have enough for their own lamps if they share. The wise virgins with oil tell the silly virgins who managed to bring lamps without oil[24] that they must go out and get it on their own. Many people wonder why the smart virgins didn't share or why the group couldn't just hang around one light. Did they really need ten lamps? Just how dark is this road?

This parable doesn't make much sense unless you know what the first-century Jewish people thought of lamps and oil when Jesus was imparting the tale. Scripture equates lamps with the Word of G: "Thy word is a lamp unto my feet." So all ten virgins had the Word of G; in fact, a great many people have the Word of G available to them. Here's

---

[24] It really is the equivalent of carrying a flashlight with no batteries. What is the point? Why did they bother bringing empty lamps in the first place?

the kicker—oil is the equivalent of good deeds and good works. The Word of G is very powerful, but it can't do its good if the people won't do good with it. You have to know what to do in order to do it. So you need the lamp. But a lamp without good deeds is nothing more than a flashlight without batteries. It's like having a space shuttle with no fuel. Sure, the potential is limitless, but absent the ability to put it into use, the shuttle is only a paperweight.

There simply must be good deeds to light the lamp. There will come a time in history and throughout history when various people will jump up and condemn others for failing to abide by Scripture. You will hear that various actions and practices are sin and that the sinner should be appropriately condemned. While every human will sin, sin is never an excuse to hate. Humans always forget that when you hear the Word of G, when you hear the Scripture, the very next questions should be, "Where is the love? Where is the good?" If someone comes to you in the name of G and begins to condemn others, pause and reflect on the message. If someone is sinning, you don't use judgment and force to stop the sin. Forcing Scripture in isolation of love on anyone is the equivalent of beating a man with a dead flashlight. He may learn the divine standard of right from wrong, but he won't want to walk with you on a dark night.

Lucifer attempted to trick Jesus by properly quoting scripture. Lucifer asks Jesus to jump off the temple—after all, G would "command the angels concerning him so that he would not even strike his foot on a stone." Lucifer was correct in his quote of Psalm 91. See, even demons can access scripture. What Lucifer lacked was the oil—the good deeds that bring the lamp to life. Lucifer wielded the dead flashlight.

Equally, had Jesus jumped, there would have been no love, no good in the action. It would have served only to allow Jesus to prove to Lucifer who he was. Jesus didn't need to prove to anyone who he was. Of course, Scripture also that states that you should not test G. Jesus properly called that one out. Human laws have similar nuances. People often claim Scripture contradicts itself, but it doesn't. There is common sense that is ingrained in every passage, but most importantly, there is love.

Ah! Lucifer. Everyone knows Lucifer. His name pops up quite frequently. He is a fallen angel. Don't think of him as the red guy with a pitchfork, tail, and horns.[25] He was quite beautiful and had an amazing singing voice. Don't get me wrong. He was no Gabriel, but his voice was still phenomenal. Lucifer had a bit of a tough time with the whole loving-everyone-equally thing. Let me digress for a moment to touch on the subject of love before I continue with the rebellion of Ole Luci.

G taught humans how they should love. G gave millions of examples that most mothers will recognize. Fathers will know this as well, but it gets complicated for someone who can barely conjugate verbs to flip between the mother and the father, so I will stay with the mother. Feel free to insert the word *father* wherever you see *mother* if that aids in your story interpretation.

When a baby is born, the mother knows and loves the baby. She has felt the baby stir within her. Her heart was touched before the baby ever breathed its first breath. When the baby is born, it knows and loves the mother. For the next year or so, the baby may not be able to articulate its needs, but it knows Mom. The baby loves Mom. There is no need for words. It is understood. The mom provides warmth, food, protection. It is just known. The mother realizes that this being has reached deep into her very heart and will turn her whole world upside down. This woman understands now what really matters in life. It isn't the money, the prestige, or the power. The mother has the same dependency on the child that the child has on her. It's love.

In fact, ask a parent of a baby who has died at childbirth. They cry, they mourn for someone they just met. How? It is the developing love for the being that was created within. It is the same love that G has for humans. Humans aren't pets, zoo animals, or experiments gone awry. They are G's children. They are loved entirely and completely by G. More than a mother with her infant child, G loved you before you were born.

That's the miracle of love; it is love in its purest, nonjudgmental form. The baby doesn't give the mother anything physical. The baby won't buy anything or flatter her. On the same note, when babies are

---

[25] Lucifer has also never played hockey for New Jersey.

born, they don't care about the frivolous stuff. The babies don't care about the parents' looks, accolades, jobs, titles, or the types of cars they drive. They want to simply be in the presence of their moms and dads. Parents, out of pure love, provide the basics of food, water, clothing, safety, and cleanliness. Humans actually have to *teach* their children that the basics are not enough. Humans foster the hunger for more than the simple. Humans teach and learn to care about the hollow, empty stuff. They spend the formative years of their children's lives encouraging their children to pursue the tangible and physical, then the children spend the rest of their lives trying to get back to the contented state of simple, innter peace.

Jesus states that one needs to approach heaven like a child. But just as G showed us what love should be in the relationship between people such as a baby and a mom, G also gave us a reflection of what happens when you focus your love on *yourself*. Too much pride grows inside. This metamorphosis is easily recognized by any parent whose loving child has changed into an adolescent. For those of you who didn't know, Lucifer was the equivalent of a fifteen-year-old when he started his defiant tirade. That fact shouldn't surprise too many parents.

The rebellion started small. He sang psalms and praises. But after a while, he didn't sing to celebrate; he sang so others would hear his voice. Kind acts were not actually committed to improve or assist others, but rather to glorify Lucifer. When other angels received compliments, Lucifer made snide comments about them to ensure that he held the highest respect among the angels. He felt that any time someone else received praise, he was made lesser. He could not comprehend the fact that a candle loses none of its light when it lights another candle. He failed to see that when you enlighten others, you all stay well-lit. He viewed relationships more as a hierarchy whereby he had to be on top. He began to expect to be loved without having to reciprocate. No happiness came if the other angels complimented him, but lack of compliments was an affront. He began to wonder what made G so much better than him. He believed he would be a better ruler than G ever could be. On more than one occasion, you could hear his silky voice shouting, "You're not the boss of me!" G totally gets what it is like to be the parent of a defiant teen, except G experiences it with angels and humans alike.

Lucifer, like many humans, began to resent when he was not the center of attention. There are millions of angels. If every angel or even every human had to be the center of attention, it would be chaos.

By keeping goodness and love as the center, G was, in essence, the nucleus of a very complex atom. Therefore, the rest of creation could happily do its part in the larger cosmos of the atom. If every proton, neutron, and electron demanded to be the nucleus, the very essence of the atom would be compromised. In fact, a proton which fails to understand the overall atom will never believe in a nucleus … of that I am positive, haha. There must be understanding of the larger picture before a human will cultivate faith in G.

Humans, especially hormonal teenagers, often enter a similar phase of defiance and rebel against G. It is a pretty normal phase and rather predictable among humans. Ultimately, you should grow out of that phase and develop into an adult who realizes that your parents weren't entirely crazy—or even if they were, understandably so. You may even start to develop understanding of parental behavior. Much like an evolved teenager, this understanding and a sudden epiphany of humility should improve your relationship with G.

The parent relationship is critical in revealing the relationship with G. A cursory review of the Ten Commandments highlights this. G begins with the directive to focus on the divine first. Immediately following the commandments to focus on the divine is the command to honor parents.

Parenthood provides a great analogy for faith, as well. A lot of atheists center their arguments on the speculative nature of the afterlife, its lack of scientific support. They build hollow temples on mountains of despair arguing that absent proof to their satisfaction, G can't exist. But G isn't a tangible teacup floating around in a distant galaxy. G isn't an item at which to point. G is a party with whom you relate, much like a parent.

Imagine if you will a conversation between a person who has a child and a person who is expecting her first child. The motivating parent may tell the expectant parent, "Oh, you are going to have such a wonderful experience with the child! Love, love, love your child. You will not believe how a child will complete your life. The child will change your life and you will find joy you could never imagine." The expectant parent may refute that belief and state that she doesn't believe it will be rewarding; it will only be work and self-sacrifice.

The motivator may then say that the expectant parent should love the child because of potential benefits, such as that child selecting the parent's nursing home in later years. The expectant parent may again refute the position, arguing that her future is already prepared and the future is simply not a concern.

Resorting to the final position, the motivator may now address the detriments by stating that the expectant parent needs to be somewhat attentive to the child or else the Department of Child Services will step in and potentially terminate the relationship entirely.

Just like a human's relationship with G, joy and love is found in the *relationship* that is created. Yes, there are positive future benefits and the need to avoid negative repercussions. But believing in G isn't necessarily for the benefits that may be obtained (heaven) or the fear of repercussion (hell) any more than relating to family is about nursing-home selection or avoiding the Department of Child Services. It is about the change that occurs within each person's heart. It is about the now. It is about the love. Everything else is peripheral.

There are parents who have done unconscionable acts to their children under the argument that the parent possesses the right to behave in such an atrocious manner. Reasonable people know that such abuses should never occur. The thought of abolishing all parenthood because of the bad actors would be absurd. On the same note, there are believers of various faiths who behave in ways that deviate from the will of G. Atheists have argued that religion should be abolished because of those deviants who perform atrocities in the name of G, but you can't dismiss the entire premise of faith because of the bad actions of those who mistakenly or even intentionally apply false "Christian" labels to bad actions, any more than you could abolish parenthood due to bad-acting parents.

Now consider the response if the expectant parent were to look at the motivator and say, "Prove it. Prove all you say about that relationship." The motivator may feel stumped. How would those with deep, innocent, and pure love for their children prove it? Aside from the changes in the life of the motivator and the kindness displayed and heralded by the motivator—the full impact of the relationship must be sought and felt. Can anyone prove to someone the deep love and compassion he or she has for another? At some point, the other person will just have to see the amazing change *in the person* as evidence that something amazing has developed. How can anyone prove love?

But that is exactly what G is and gives. G doesn't just foster love between the individual and G, but between the individual and all of humanity. Like a parent should, G loves all the children and equally expects the children to share that love with one another. Sharing the love fulfills the one who loves; it also should comfort the one who feels unloved. G expects all children to love one another. The result of this expectation is that even when people grow up without ever experiencing the deep parental love that should have been provided, there are others out there who *do* love them for who they are. They love not for what the others have done or will do, but unconditionally for who they are now. This is the expectation of G, to show the deepest love possible to everyone. Once you know how much G loves you as an individual, you learn how much G loves every person. You learn to love G. You then can't help but love other people because you can't possibly hate something that G treasures if you love G.

There is no one beyond love. Sure, there are sinners, but that is a limited pool containing only … well, every human. So there is no excuse for not loving a sinner. Besides, the role of G is pretty big and should not be assumed by mere mortals. Leave the driving to us and the judging to G.

A great number of humans have attributed fault to newborn babies, arguing that they are born into original sin. Babies don't *know* good from bad. Adults *teach* them. But babies are, just like adults, born with the ability to learn and act on the bad. Scripture states that *all* fall short of the glory of G. Children are not inferior on this point, but superior. Jesus stated, "Let the children come to me and do not hinder them, for the kingdom of G belongs to such as these. I tell the truth, anyone who will not receive the kingdom of G like a little child will never enter it." Babies are born trusting, loving, dependent, and humble; it takes a lot of work to screw up those divine traits with worldly values. Babies got it right; they just can't tell you how they did it.

> G blessed them and said to them, "Be fruitful and increase in number …"

Ah, the first two commands to people.[26] Here G directs the humans to be fruitful and increase. First and foremost, humans are to bear good fruit—develop the habit and character of doing going deeds. After the art of love is mastered, or at least initiated, then procreate. G doesn't expect people to crank out litters of children like hamsters gone wild. G expects people to learn how to act out of love and then increase the number of people who are being raised to do the same thing. If all humans disciplined themselves to truly love other people *before* they had children and then raised the children to the same standard, imagine how amazing the world would be!

Second, "increase in number" does involve two people. I know some humans argue man was originally androgynous, one body both male and female, but that would make reproduction completely devoid of intimacy. In fact, one-body reproducing was left to simpler classifications of creation such as amoebas. There is no relationship or connection in asexual reproduction. Also, it would be weird to have to tell an asexual thing to multiply with itself.

G was clear that a male and a female were created. G is all about relationships. That is how we learn to love and develop patience and tolerance. G frequently equates his love for humans to that of a husband for a wife. There is relationship. It is hard to have a relationship in one body— unless you are schizophrenic, and then it just depends on the quality of the other personalities dwelling within.

---

[26] Yes, the first two commandments, not one. There is an *and* in there.

Also, two heads are better than one when it comes to conversing, relating, intimating, being fruitful, and doing math—or multiplying.

It's funny how humans never thought to suggest that all of the animals were asexual when G told them to multiply; yet the same command was given to human and scholars jump to the belief that man was asexual or somehow encouraged to reproduce with oneself. Odd. G said there were more than one, and "they" were "male" and "female." G was not vague or ambiguous.

Humankind performed as directed. There is a deeper concept to be explored here. I don't want to take anything away from the command. G was clear. But consider this: the primary directive is to be fruitful—aka be good, do good. Increase in number applies not only to population but also to the good works. Don't do one good deed and then sit back on your laurels. Multiply the good deeds.

> "Fill the earth and subdue it. Rule over the fish of the sea and the birds of the air and over every living creature that moves and creeps on the ground."

G gave humans dominion over creeps. So ladies, think of all those crazy dates you have had with creepy guys and take solace in the fact that G gave you dominion over those creeps too. Unfortunately, it is a right not exercised often enough.

Humans began to fill the earth, as directed.

This whole "rule over" thing is important. It doesn't mean to boss around, bully, or oppress. After all, how could you bully a bird or a fish? To rule means to take responsibility for and to care for.[27] G gave people dominion over the animals so that humans would care for them in the same way G was caring for people in Eden. It is important to understand *dominion* here. G was not intending humans to rule as they will eventually interpret the word "rule." It is not a question of power. G wanted people to rule with the same compassion, dedication to creating, and love for life as G ruled. People tend to think that ruling means being served. In truth, the one in power should be

---

[27] You may be the ruler of your dog, but you are also the one picking up the poop.

the servant. The history of the word *rule* actually means "to stoop on bended knee."[28] The one in power needs to think of the well-being of all. This concept got lost somewhere in time.

> Then G said "I give you every seed-bearing plant on the face of the whole earth and every tree that has fruit with seed in it. They will be yours for food. And to all the beasts of the earth and all the birds of the air and all the creatures that move on the ground—everything that has the breath of life in it—I give every green plant for food."
>
> And it was so.
>
> G saw all that G had made, and it was very good.

Ah, the "very good." Up until now, G's adjective was only "good." More important, most people don't realize that the Hebrew for "very good" is *tov me-od*. Interestingly enough, *tov* means the inclination for good, while *me-od* is the inclination for the opposite. *Tov me-od* means creation was made "very good," but it also means made with an "inclination towards good and the opposite of good."

There is old lore that sums this up nicely. It speaks of a man who approaches a priest and tells the priest that two tigers fight within his spirit; one is good, the other is not. He is afraid. He asks the priest which tiger will prevail when they fight. The priest calmly replies that the tiger that prevails is the one the man feeds. Knowing the bad tiger is there should motivate people to work hard at training, feeding, and caring for the good tiger.

G created people with the inclination for both with the hope that humans would pursue and *choose* the good. Granted, some primal urges are bound to surface—especially in the act of multiplying. But G made people complete, with all inclinations and the free will and ability to balance them appropriately.

> And there was off, and there was on—the sixth day.

This sentence concludes what you humans have labeled Genesis 1. G didn't number verses. When you read Genesis 1; it is important

---

[28] Thereby making it easier to pick up poop.

to note that Eden is never mentioned. There is a good reason for this: Genesis 1 refers to the creation of the *earth*. Eden comes next. Eden is a place *within* the earth, a location, a city if you will. Kind of like when humans buy a home, and then they go and put a flower bed in one corner. The house was built in Genesis 1, and the garden planted in Genesis 2.

Another distinguishing trait between Genesis 1 and Genesis 2 is that in Genesis 1, you do not see the name Adam, nor will you see reference to man in the singular.[29] Man*kind* was created in Genesis 1, and as Scripture notes, this includes women. This explains why, in later verses, Adam and Eve's child, Cain, feared that people would kill him. Where did those people come from? Whom did Cain and Seth marry? It's easy—see Genesis 1. G made humans, G made "them."

Some human scholars argue that the order of creation in Genesis 1 conflicts with that of Genesis 2. It doesn't. The Bible can be read in harmony. When two verses of Scripture *appear* to be in conflict, there is some reflection that may need to occur in order to get to the truth. Often, the only true conflict is the false presumptions humans present in their analysis. Genesis 2 doesn't change any of the creation events as they have occurred; it simply tells of something more specific that happened. For instance, if a man says he married five women, then later says he has only one wife—the average human may claim there is a discrepancy. But if the humans are informed that the man in question is a minister, it becomes clear there is no conflict. He has married five women—to other men. He gave himself to one.

Scholars also argue that Genesis 1 and Genesis 2 contrast what G intended versus what actually happened. G doesn't make mistakes. G can't suggest there was a way G intended to make people but defaulted to another method because of the inherent flaws of the material with which G was working. There is no Humankind 2.0.

The only way these passages conflict is if you presuppose that Adam, the one particular man, was created on the *sixth* day. If you begin with that position, then Scripture will not reconcile. If you get

---

[29] Except for that one crazy reference that you have simmering on the back burner whereby G made reference to creating "him," new clause, and "them, male and female."

off that mark, or that Adam, and properly read the events in Genesis 2 as *timing* for the creation of Adam (one man) on the third day, but *humans* on the sixth day, then there is no conflict.

Act 2: Genesis 2, The Creation, More Specifically

Thus the heavens and the earth were completed in their entire vast array.

Most people miss the poignancy of the fact that the heavens and earth were completed. Was heaven incomplete before? It wasn't incomplete in the sense that heaven lacked some critical puzzle piece. Think of heaven more as a large home with many rooms. The house can be fully built, with all the rooms complete in exquisite detail, but you have to add loving family, guests, children, and others to fill those rooms. The building itself was finished, but only after the rooms were filled with people to love was it complete.

Also note that earth is not separate from heaven: it is *within* heaven. Earth is the happy baby in a mansion with many rooms and whose laughter is heard echoing in the halls. Heaven is everywhere. It is within each person. It is not out of reach, and it is not some futuristic goal to be obtained after death. It is the now, the was, and the will be, not *just* the will be. When humans behave with the concept that heaven can be obtained only after death, they miss so much of life.

> By the seventh day G had finished the work; so on the seventh day G rested from all work. And G blessed the seventh day and made it holy, because G rested from all the work of creating that had been done.

This whole Sabbath thing is critical. For those people who can't seem to stop *doing* on a daily basis, for those people who can't take some short time to give thanks and admire all the beauty around them, for those people G provides a weekly opportunity to get it right. So if you can't seem to figure out that you get a new chance to start over every morning, maybe starting over weekly will serve you well. The Sabbath serves as a reminder that all that worldly stuff you do throughout the week isn't going to complete you. Humans get to stop pretending to create and to revel in the created instead. Humans need to pause, back up, and reflect on what is truly eternal and valuable. They also get to sleep in late.

> This is the account of the heavens and the earth when they were created, when the Lord G made the earth and the heavens.

Here is the next most notable change between Genesis 1 and 2. Now, you will see the word *Lord* prefacing the reference to G. Hmm ... why?

Well, G's name is holy. It is sacred. *Lord*, or Adonai, is the most frequently used name for G in the Bible. The meaning of the name of G is provided in Exodus—"I am who I am." This was pronounced "Yahveh." The Jewish people, who had the original text of the Bible on scrolls, were very good about keeping the sacred name holy. Tradition bestowed the right to say the holy name only to the high priest. After the destruction of the second temple, the scribes would flag the name of the *Lord* in the scrolls so as to remind the reader to honor its holiness and not to state it aloud. Later, the Masoretes, who vocalized the Hebrew text, read the name Adonai in conjunction with the reminder not to say it out loud ... a bit of irony there. The resulting pronunciation came out as *JEHOVAH*.

The word *Lord* is here to indicate that something holy is happening. In Genesis 1, G builds, creates, and implements a structure

Act 2: Genesis 2, The Creation, More Specifically 37

on a grand scheme. Genesis 2 takes you off the big picture of general creation to accomplish a specific task. Genesis 1 is the architect and general-contractor work. Genesis 2 is the sculptor.

> Now no shrub had yet appeared on the earth and no plant had yet sprung up, for the Lord G had not sent rain on the earth and there was no one to work the ground, but streams came up from the earth and watered the whole surface of the ground. Then the Lord G formed a man from the dust of the ground and breathed into his nostrils the breath of life, and the man became a living being.

This paragraph contains so much information. The most important bit of information is a *time frame*. This section mentions how water covered the earth, and *then* man (singular) was made from the dust. In order to get dust, land and water must separate. Think about the time when the water and land were separated and there were not yet plants or vegetation. If you go back and look at the chronology of creation in Genesis 1, you will find this occurred *on the third day*. Nothing in the order of creation stated in Genesis 1 has changed—people were still created on the sixth day—but something apart from the general creation happens on the third day.

The third day has pretty rich significance, spiritually speaking. It will come to prove very significant in the events of the Messiah. The number three, in general, has rich scriptural meaning. Whenever you see the number three in Scripture, G isn't just telling you about a finite number of things; G is telling you to pay attention because something substantial, solid, and related to divine perfection and salvation is occurring. For example, Jonah was in the belly of a fish for three days, there were three sons from Noah after the flood, Moses was hidden by his mom for three months, Moses requested a three-day journey into the wilderness, Jesus' ministry lasted three years, Mary stayed with Elizabeth for three months, Jesus was missing in the temple for three days, Saul was blinded for three days.[30] I could go on, but there is a story to tell.

The third day, the Lord G made a man. Here is where G made *one* man. Remember that quote on the back burner? "In the image of G, G created him; male and female G created them." This sentence has two distinct different clauses and two distinct creations. One creation was a "him" on the third day and the other creation a "them," on the sixth.

If you review the chronology of creation in Genesis 1, you will notice that on days one through three, G creates many things, but the *purpose* for the creation is not stated. After G created Adam on the third day, G identifies the specific purpose identified on the fourth day. The fourth day contains a purpose as G states that the lights were created to "serve as signs to mark sacred times."[31] As you will see later in my story, all the sacred times point to the Messiah.

G made Adam on the third day. Being all-knowing, G had then set in motion the birth, death, and coming again of the Messiah by the fourth day. This means that when G made Adam, G also devised the entire salvation of mankind by the end of the next day. This isn't without merit; Adam and the Messiah are frequently juxtapositioned[32] against one another as one man ushered sin into the world and the other ushered in the kingdom of G.

This section also mentions that the Lord G breathed into Adam's nostrils the "breath of life." The book of Timothy tells you what G's breath is and why it is. "Scripture is G-breathed and is useful for teaching, rebuking, correcting and training in righteousness." As when Paul wrote this, the only recognized Scripture at that time was the Old Testament.[33] Adam received the Word of G directly from

---

[30] Mathematically speaking, two straight lines cannot enclose any space; three are needed to form a plane figure. Two plane surfaces cannot form a solid; you need three dimensions to form a solid. Literally speaking, it took three little pigs to build a house to code, three bears to scare a girl, and three blind mice to scare a knife-wielding farm worker.

[31] You can take that little point off the back burner now.

[32] No, juxtaposition is not a ballet move.

[33] The New Testament was a work in progress.

the source. G's Word gave life. It still does. It is the ultimate truth for humans. This will, naturally, lead to the question of "What is truth?"

G's Word is truth. It is inerrant and timeless. It cracks me up when people say there is no such thing as truth, because if their statement is true, they will have just proven themselves wrong. Truth exists regardless of what people say. You can be as philosophical as you would like, but that doesn't change the existence of truth. It is by seeking the truth that one can attain wisdom. As G's word is truth, respect for the word is the first step to enlightenment. This is not as complicated as most people think.

G states, "A man's words are deep waters but wisdom is a babbling brook."[34] You could argue forever about whether or not a lake exists, but when all the debate has settled, you will still come out wet. True wisdom can be ingested and absorbed and is quenching. It is not the murky philosophical depths that few ever frequent and where none can survive.

You can contemplate deep and profound thoughts. Your conversation can become poetry as you break down each mystery of life and reduce everything to nothingness. But once your conversation has ended, have your conclusions enhanced your life or the lives of others?

People will even argue that they cannot prove their own existence. If you are struggling with proving your *own* existence, perhaps, it may not be the best time to undertake analyzing the existence of greater than yourself.

> Now G had planted a garden in the east, in Eden; and there G put the man G had formed. And G made all kinds of trees grow out of the ground—trees that were pleasing to the eye and good for food. In the middle of the garden were the Tree of Life and the Tree of the Knowledge of Good and Evil.[35]

Ladies and gentlemen, we have now formally shifted our attention from the entire earth to simply that of the garden. G put the

---

[34] You can read this in Proverbs. Proverbs are the writings G imparted to Solomon. They are actually bumper stickers here in heaven.

[35] G also created the Tree of Polka Music and the Tree of the Art of Mime. While man could eat from those, they were generally avoided by most.

garden in the east of Eden. Humans always forget this part. G put a garden in Eden. Eden is not a garden; Eden *contains* a garden. The earth is not Eden. The earth contains Eden and its garden.

It is interesting that the garden is in the east. There is a great deal of significance with the east. Scripture will foreshadow of Messiah coming from the east. I bring this up pretty much as foreshadowing, I think; I guess I can't tell you what is about to happen when it has already happened. Back to the Tree of the Knowledge of Good and Evil and the Tree of Life.[36]

Proverbs explains the Tree of Life. It represents wisdom. The Tree of the Knowledge of Good and Evil represents knowledge. There is a huge difference between the two. Like the old saying goes, "Knowledge knows that a tomato is a fruit. Wisdom knows better than to put a tomato in a fruit salad." I have knowledge of the quadratic equation taught in many a calculus course. Even as an angel, I lack the wisdom to understand when or why I would ever need to invoke such a formula. Knowledge, absent wisdom, can be cruel and heartless. Knowledge allows you to manipulate consequences—or at least delay them—instead of exercising self-control. Knowledge gives you verifiable data absent appropriate context.

Wisdom compels you to see the greater picture; how things interrelate so that the greater good is achieved. When you analyze how actions affect the broader scope, you can't help but do good deeds. You can't help but love other people. You can't help but help. You begin to appreciate the relationships between and among *everyone and everything*. You will appreciate the relationships as a satiating source of happiness. The fruit of the Tree of Life is good deeds.

Conversely, knowledge looks in isolation at a *specific* purpose, how other things may affect one particular thing. When you analyze how actions affect you personally, you fall onto self-centered actions. You pursue the things that bring your personal satisfaction. You can't help but become defensive. You focus on how everything relates to *you*, specifically. You desire and pursue pleasures to try to satiate your personal hungers. Remember that fruit is intended to help others, not to benefit the tree producing. Bearing fruit for yourself

---

[36] Sadly, not polka playing and mime

will always leave you hungry. The Fruit of the Tree of Knowledge of Good and Evil is pride.

One of the great deceptions that will overtake humans is the belief that they should do whatever makes them happy or whatever they feel like doing. This thought process is akin to eating anything that makes you full. Eating absolutely anything may fill you up, but it may not make you healthy. You can eat a dozen doughnuts, five chocolate cakes, a cup of nuts and bolts and cyanide. You will feel full; you will not feel good. In fact, you won't feel much at all with that last addition to the menu. The standard is not what you *want* to do; the standard should be what *needs* to be done. The standard is not how any one action improves your personal state (knowledge); but how any one action improves the bigger picture (wisdom).

> A river watering the garden flowed from Eden; from there it was separated into four headwaters. The name of the first is the Pishon; it winds through the entire land of Havilah, where there is gold. (The gold of that land is good; aromatic resin and onyx are also there.) The name of the second river is the Gihon; it winds through the entire land of Cush. The name of the third river is the Tigris; it runs along the east side of Ashur. And the fourth river is the Euphrates.

Upon cursory review, humans may read over this section as if it were a mere geography lesson. Ah, but G is so much smarter than that. Every time you read something in Scripture, you should always ask yourself, why is this here? Whether in history, the present, or the future,[37] there are millions of events that have transpired but only a select few are mentioned in Scripture. Granted, G does put many historical facts in Scripture to provide evidence of accuracy, but there is always a deeper meaning to the words.

This particular verse is interesting as the etymology[38] of the names will reveal things. I won't get too deep into the discussion of the background of the words as the only people the discussion would

---

[37] Like I can keep any of them straight …

[38] This is a fancy word for the history and historical translations of words. It is also the study of etymos.

benefit would be insomniacs; but I will tell you enough to make it interesting.

The name of the first river, Pishon, means "to be strong, increase, and spread." Interesting choice of name, given G's command to multiply. This river winds through Havilah, which can be broken down into a few derivations but ultimately means "exhausted revelation." That's just funny if you really think about it.

The name of the second river, Gihon, means to "burst forth," much like a child being born. This river runs through the land of Cush, which, strangely enough, can mean "as if he were weak" or "as if he were getting smarter." If you happen to know what Adam will do with the forbidden fruit, it is safe to say he successfully became weak and smarter at the same time.

The name of the third river, Tigris, more commonly known as the Haddakel, means "sharp" and "rapid." Some derivations of the definition include "to prick," "to sting in order to split," and "to separate." The Tigris runs through the land of Asshur, also known as Assyria, which means "level plain." Good and evil will now be leveled within man, whereas before the fruit eating, man knew only good. And while I don't want to break chronology—after the fruit incident, there will be a split between humans and G, specifically, and among humans generally.[39]

An interesting geological split is the fact that the area surrounding Jordan and Israel is on a great rift, tectonically speaking. In a sense, the land had a major fault. Later chapters in Genesis will tell you that in the days of Peleg,[40] the earth was divided. This division caused a major change in river flow, so much so that in later years only two of the four rivers will be readily identifiable ... although their courses will be somewhat different than in days of yore—er, *now*.

If I really wanted to go off on a geology lesson, I could show you how the flow of all these rivers can be logically, scientifically, and scripturally traced back to prove that Eden rested around the area of

---

[39] Another split that will occur involves the flaming sword that will eventually appear in the story. This sword will split spirit and soul and reach into your very heart.

[40] Not to be confused with Peg Leg, a fictional pirate.

Jerusalem. Jerusalem really is a big hangout for G, kind of a home-court advantage thing.

The fourth river is the Euphrates, or properly known as the Parat. *Parat* means "to bear fruit" or "to be fruitful." This is the ultimate request of G, to do good and to be happy doing good. This is bearing fruit. It is by following this last path that humans will be able to return to Eden.[41]

> G took the man and put him in the garden of Eden to work it and take care of it. And G commanded the man, "You are free to eat from any tree in the garden; but you must not eat from the Tree of the Knowledge of Good and Evil, for when you eat from it you will certainly die."

It is important to note that G indicated man was to *work* the garden and take care of it. Most people don't realize that G did not create humans to lounge around and have birds carry bunches of grapes to their outstretched arms while they reclined on soft grass. G recognized that humans need to utilize their bodies and work the physical in addition to the spiritual. Man was not intended to be only spiritual. There was actual labor involved. In fact, there is spiritual benefit derived from the physical labor associated with working and taking care of things.

I also need to provide clarity here on what *die* means. It is actually quite a big deal when you are immortal. We angels appreciate the magnitude of the threat of finiteness. To die is equated to becoming mortal.[42]

You've got to admit that as far as consequences go, this is a pretty big one. It's not like G said, "Side effects include weight gain, rashes, blurred vision, loss of hearing, muscle spasms, drowsiness, and a tendency to crave Brussels sprouts." No, G said they would die.

In fact, death not only encompassed mortality, it also brought forth natural atrophy. Have you ever heard a human say something

---

[41] Bearing fruit, not physically following the river.

[42] It is also the equivalent of a singular cube with little dots on it, but that's not important right now.

like "Why bother making my bed? It is just going to get messed up again." or "Why bothering cleaning? It's just going to get dirty again." or "Why bother bathing? I'm just going to get stinky again." or "Why bother eating? I'm just going to get hungry again." At some point, the ludicrousness of the perspective sets in. Everything naturally decays, rots, rusts if left unattended. Leave metal outside, leave an apple on the counter, leave a shirt in the grass—the very substance begins to erode, to break down. The things you care for must be cared for. You must work for the things you love.

A human's spirit is the same way. It needs to have attention or it will start to decompose. It becomes callused, cold, selfish, perverted, or cynical when left to its own devices. Whenever humans witness an atrocity, perversion, or violence, the response should not be to harden over and allow anger to fester until it boils into hatred, apathy, or fear. The response is to fight the decay of morality by showing more love and more compassion. It is those who have championed love who have allowed the world to persevere as long as it will come to last. It is those who fought against the natural inclination of violence or apathy who have given hope to the world.

You know, we angels get to be in all sorts of places. Sometimes it is fun to masquerade on earth as a human just to pass time (that's actually a joke since we aren't subject to it). But one question I hear frequently is, "Why would G even bother to put the tree that could lead to a fall in the garden to begin with?" G wasn't tempting or trying to entrap humans by putting a tree in the middle of the garden. In fact, G can't tempt, as temptation is bad and G is good. G wanted to make sure the humans were there by choice, not force.

If G set a buffet before you and said you could eat anything you wanted, but G put only those Brussels sprouts on the table, you would hardly have a choice. But what if G put out all sorts of different foods—fruits, vegetables, desserts, bugs, and anything else you could think about—and said to eat what you want, but then encouraged you to avoid certain foods because they may harm you physically, spiritually, or emotionally? G gives you a choice. The variety is what makes the love of G a pure choice. Now, if you eat everything G asked you not to eat, well then, you don't really have a great deal of love for G (or yourself, for that matter). But if you happily eat the *healthy* food , then your choices are evidence of your trust in G and your care for yourself.

Almost all parents will tell you, it isn't the child they control that makes them proud; it is the child who exercises self-control. G gave humans the ability to choose good or bad. Of course, this choice gave Lucifer opportunity to find company for his misery.

The tree was never evil; the tree merely presents an opportunity to learn evil. It's kind of like the whole "Guns don't kill people, people kill people" argument. The tree didn't give humans the bad; humans seeking bad went to the tree. Man, on his own volition, sought out the knowledge of bad.

If you read closely, G was quite simple and concise in the creation of the taboo. See, if G had hired an attorney to write up the requirement, it would read more like, "In exchange and consideration for immortality and eternal access to the Divine (for purposes of this clause, "eternal" includes all calendar days, business days, and holidays from the Effective Date of this Agreement (as defined elsewhere) through infinity) G, hereinafter "The Party of the First Part," hereby directs, orders, commands, and requires that the male form currently known as "Adam," but hereinafter referred to as "The Party of the Second Part," not eat, lick, taste, masticate, indulge, or otherwise attempt or actually ingest (hereinafter "Eat") that portion of the tree which produces, houses, and/or contains seeds necessary for the reproduction of the respective plant/tree and does not scientifically constitute the stem, leaves, or roots of the plant, including but not limited to bark, tendrils, etc. (hereinafter "Fruit"), of the tree, constituting real property and located at the central part of the garden region in the area commonly known as "Eden" (hereinafter "Tree of Knowledge") and further situated near and beside the tree of eternal life currently known as the "Tree of Life." Should the Party of the Second Part, whether in willful or reckless disregard for this provision, Eat of the Fruit of the Tree of Knowledge, the grant of immortality shall dissolve, and side effects will include, but are not limited to, loss of a glorified body, reduced access to the Divine, mortality, introduction of flaming swords, and headaches. The Party of the Second Part hereby represents and warrants that, as there is only one rule being enacted, said party will assume all risks of injury, illness, temptation, and inconvenience associated with a breach of this agreement. Furthermore and to wit …" I could go on, but to put it in pure legal form, I would need to reduce the font significantly and insert a preamble with plenty of *whereases* and *heretofores*. I would also need to start charging exorbitant rates. In fact, by writing so much legalese, I risk compromising my position in heaven. Eek, I need to move on.

G was short, G was concise. It is the humans that always want to extrapolate regulations, because they know some other human will try to find a loophole. A case on point involves some of those people G created on day six. I think most people know the general story of the creation, but the devil is in the details, ha-ha.

Sidebar, if you please: G has formally told Adam he cannot eat from the Tree of the Knowledge of Good and Evil. Do you notice what's missing? Woman. She won't be created for a few more verses. A key piece of evidence that should be contemplated in the charges against the woman[43] that surface later is that G didn't give her the don't-eat-the-fruit-of-the-tree-of-knowledge command.

> The LORD G said, "It is not good for the man to be alone. I will make a helper suitable for him."

G realized that there was something empty in this man. Eve wasn't created yet so this void in man cannot be attributed to her. Man was not communing with G as he should have been. The critical word in the passage is "alone." Adam was with G, how was he alone? Man needed relationship, and if he couldn't commune directly with G, then he needed to commune with someone who could "*help*" him find G. Woman would be that suitable helper. For the first time since all of creation, G declared something "not good." If all was well with Adam, G wouldn't have made those remarks. G is pretty deliberate in the communication arena.

---

[43] The woman later to be known as Eve.

The apostle Paul would later say how it is better to be celibate, better to abstain than to be married; but G said simply it was not good for man to be alone. The two texts can be read in harmony.

People need relationship with G. In the grand scheme of things, only that relationship matters. If a person is in deep communion with G, that person can continue to be single because a person in relationship with G would not be alone. If a person cannot find relationship with G or simply wants to explore G on a different level, then marry another person who can help develop or enhance the relationship with G. G isn't mandating celibacy or denouncing it. G is simply stating that *relationship with G is primary*. Relationships with other people should foster the primary relationship. Humans were not vested with the rights to demand celibacy or marriage of other humans. Instead humans are encouraged to explore their own, personal relationship with G and to understand what enhances that relationship.

But no matter how you look at it, love requires fellowship with people. The early religious people recognized this. The Jewish writing, the Talmud, would go so far as to say that "he is called a man only if he has a wife." Through time, a departure occurs from recognizing that the value of the sum of the parts is greater than the whole.[44] The union created by a man and woman is greater than either individual on their own. This focus shifted through time to believing that one in isolation can learn G better. But G is not isolation; G is fellowship. You fellowship with G *and* you fellowship with others; it is not mutually exclusive. If there are not others, then it is all about you. It is never intended to be all about any one person. Hence G's recognition that man needed a special, custom-made, divine, mail-order bride, and also that man needed general fellowship with others. One in isolation cannot multiply.

---

[44] While Aristotle brought this concept forth on a metaphysical level and Max Wertheimer Gestalt on a psychological level, I will present it on an even more digestible plane: I like eggs, I like sugar, and I like flour. I don't actually like to eat any one of those items by itself; but I really like cake. The sum is greater than the parts.

Now the LORD G had formed out of the ground all the wild animals and all the birds in the sky. G brought them to the man to see what he would name them; and whatever the man called each living creature, that was its name. So the man gave names to all the livestock, the birds in the sky and all the wild animals.

Here is yet another critical fact often overlooked by humans. Genesis 2 is often read as G searching for that helper in the animals. Not the case. Look deeper. This section is not telling you that man is looking for a helper among the animals. It is telling you the time! Recall that earlier Adam was made when water and land separated but before vegetation—hence, Day 3. What you are being told by the introduction of animals is that the story is now on day six. The mere fact that Adam is talking to animals means that he has successfully survived to day six and is possibly emulating Dr. Doolittle.

Adam used to walk along in the garden with G just talking, questioning, laughing, but there was that noticeable, slightly confrontational quirk about Adam. Clearly, he was in G's image, but he also had an undertow that subtly snuck into conversations and behaviors.

"So G, you said not to eat from the Tree of the Knowledge of Good and Evil. Well, what if a fruit fell from the tree and rolled over near another tree? Technically, I would be eating fruit from the ground, right? Or what if I ate the leaves or the bark from the tree? That isn't fruit, so it's okay to eat, right?" Loopholes—every demon's dream.

In addition to Adam's tendency toward edgy interrogatories,[45] he also has strange urges to hunt the animals. He likes to sneak up on them and wrestle them to the ground. At this time, it was rather easy, since the food chain wasn't truly in effect and the animals had no fear of humans. Some animals were easier to pin. Possums were never a challenge.

G rightfully put the fear into the animals once humans demonstrated an ability to separate themselves from good—in other words,

---

[45] Not popularly known, but true nonetheless, is that lawyers' work is the oldest profession on earth.

Act 2: Genesis 2, The Creation, More Specifically   49

the fall. Absent that gift of fear, animals would have been annihilated in the first few decades outside the garden.

Adam also engages in rather quirky behaviors, such as rounding up several animals of a particular species and racing them on enclosed tracks made from rocks. Adam loves to wager on which animal will win any given race. But rarely finding a willing human participant in the betting games, he finds himself ensuring that his selected animal always takes first place. If he bets on the cheetah—which tends to be his favorite—he will undoubtedly pit it up against a porcupine, beaver, and a trout. When he is particularly annoyed, he gives the animals stupid names.[46]

> But for Adam no suitable helper was found. So G caused the man to fall into a deep sleep; and while he was sleeping, G took one of the man's ribs and closed up the place with flesh. Then G made a woman from the rib taken out of the man, and G brought her to the man.

Animals and humans are created, because we are on Day 6, after all. But of the humans that were created, there just wasn't a good fit with Adam. Adam needed something a little more personal.

Please note that G caused Adam to sleep during the creation of Eve. Adam did not make, participate, see, or even consult with G in the creation of woman. He was oblivious to the entire event. Both Adam and the woman were created by G. One made from dust, the other from bone (made from dust), but both owe their lives solely to the Creator.

Adam is clearly impressed with this final product presented to him. He repeatedly makes advances toward woman by using cheesy pick-up lines and reminders that they need to get busy and multiply. After all, rules are rules.[47]

Woman isn't quite sure what to do with this man. She is reluctant to engage in physical activity because it feels as if there is something else that needs to happen. Throughout history, this same battle of

---

[46] Hence, the platypus, hippopotamus, and chow-chow.

[47] A time-honored tradition still practiced by many a human today.

the sexes plays out. Men seek to multiply, while women often want to flesh out the "be fruitful" command first.

You see, being fruitful, as I mentioned previously, is a symbol of good deeds. In order to be fruitful, a person must prepare by disciplining the body to commit to love before engaging in physical manifestations of love. If you discipline the body to act out of something other than love, then there will be more doubt than commitment, and humans will run the risk of having their offspring mirror this weakness.

This is one of the largest problems that plague marital relationships throughout time. Stereotypically speaking, women tend to focus on seeing overt evidence of love,[48] and men tend to focus on the physical act of multiplying. Both are necessary to fulfill G's command. It's important that each person addresses different aspects to ensure that neither is left out; it is a healthy yin-yang thing.

Two people focusing on only the physical would eventually find themselves devoid of spiritual intimacy and the commitment that love can bring. They can also be easily sidetracked by competing physical factors, namely other multiplication factors.

Two people focused only on good works may also find themselves devoid of a different kind of intimacy, as there would be little to bond two people who lack the physical connection. The partners may begin to feel that they are just like every other person and there is nothing special or unique between them.

Ideally, both math and fruitfulness happen. G did not say to "*go forth* and multiply." G said to "*be fruitful* and multiply." Humans need to discipline themselves and their lives so they produce healthy fruit before they generate offspring. If they do not have firm self-control of their lives, thoughts, and actions, they will perpetuate these negative traits. Humans need to be able to model a G-centered life, not a human-centered life.

I hear many a man complain that the woman he is dating is always pushing to get married. Funny thing, this pressure is commonly found where there is physical intimacy. The man is able to multiply, and the woman simply pushes for overt evidence of love. If men don't want to be pressured, don't do math.

---

[48] i.e. Commitment, compassion, care, carats.

It is just as difficult for a man to go long periods without multiplying as it is for a woman to go without some evidence or assurance of love. Not to be unfair to men, I see many a woman withhold the math as leverage. Math is a gift that is meant to be explored. It is very important to many men. They are pretty basic creatures, and math is one clear way for the woman to solve a problem.

Being fruitful and multiplying go hand in hand. If you are in a relationship and one of these is missing, think … is the other missing too? If so, do your part and bring it forth. See how long it takes before your mate starts catching up. Sometimes all it takes is for someone to take the first step.

Interesting enough, there is Jewish writing that states that G shall be with every man and woman joined together. The words for "man and woman" are AISH VASHH; the word for G is "IH". If the couple leads such a life as to push G away, the "I" from the word "AISH" and the "H" from "VASHH" are taken away and thus IH, or G, departs. The remaining words become ASH VASH which means "fire and fire." The message is simple: keep G at the forefront of the relationship and you won't get burned.

If you are frustrated in your relationship, or cannot reach the point where you feel you can appropriately show love, then wait before multiplying. Human frustration will not lessen unless the fruitfulness increases. G must be present to develop fruitfulness. Fruitfulness must precede consummation because consummation leads to offspring.

Children are a manifestation of the love you shared with one another; they are evidence of G's love for you. They are gifts, not burdens. If you see the child as something that *takes away* from you and not something that *gives* to you; then you are not in a fruitful mind-set. Love is a product of multiplication. That is the beauty of love—it only multiplies; it does not divide or subtract. When someone has their first child, they love it so much. When they have their second, they do not divide that love in half or thirds or fourths. The love multiplies, thereby fulfilling the command to multiply. *That is all love knows how to do*; it is the essence of multiplication.

Adam said, "This is now bone of my bones and flesh of my flesh; she shall be called 'woman,' for she was taken out of man."

For this reason a man will leave his father and mother and be united to his wife, and they will become one flesh.

Adam was delighted with this woman. Boy, was he delighted! Think about it. It was said that man will leave his parents and become so close with his wife that they will be one.

One point worth noting is that having come from his side, woman was equal with man in character. She was not taken from his feet, to be thought inferior. She was not taken from his head, to be considered superior. She was not taken from his arm to be thought humorous. Sorry, bad joke.

The apostle Paul would later point out that while original man was formed by G, from there on out every other man comes from a woman. This is an important point. If men debase women, then—as a product of a woman—they would be that much more inferior. Everyone is brought equally into the world.

Another interesting point is what is not said. You are given insight as to Adam's opinion, but you never hear how the woman felt. The fact that you don't know what she is thinking will play into events that later transpire. Don't be so rash as to assume that Adam was this woman's knight in shining armor. After all, they just met.

Notice that there was no mandate of hierarchy. All answered directly to G. Many people believe that by virtue of being created first Adam had authority over the woman later to be known as Eve. G never said or did anything to suggest that. Sure, Adam *called* her "woman."[49] Notice the choice of word is *called*, not named. He doesn't formally *name* her until after the fall. Naming indicates authority. Adam did not get to *name* Eve at her creation as he did not yet have authority. He *called* her woman, but he *named* her Eve.

The man and his wife were both naked, and they felt no shame

—much like those dolphins.

---

[49] Aka "Man 2.0"

Act 3: Genesis 3, The Fall

You know, I have been telling you a story that is already written down. I am merely recounting the story in Genesis, the first book of the Old Testament—the current testament if you're Jewish. I suppose my actions are a bit redundant, but I always thought it intriguing to add some background to the text. I guess you could say that I am giving you the inside scoop of the events, an angelic *Entertainment Weekly*, if you will. Of course, even things clearly written down get misinterpreted and misapplied. It is interesting how humans can read the story and miss details or select those details that best support a particular ideology. That's why I'm here to remind you that G has always intended Scripture to be interpreted in favor of love. When in doubt, choose life and choose love.

> Now the serpent was more crafty than any of the wild animals the LORD G had made. He said to the woman, "Did G really say, 'You must not eat from any tree in the garden?'"

You know, many people think there was an actual snake, much like the one in the cartoon version of *The Jungle Book*, twirling around a tree, hissing and poking his pointy little tongue in the woman's ear.

There was a snake, all right, but not the traditional kind.[50] It was part of a particular unruly angel. The part of him that enacted the temptation was snakelike. It slithered in his mouth and hissed out suggestions. To this day, all humans possess this snake and must learn to subdue it. More sin comes from a human's snake than any other body part.

The apostle James will later state, "All kinds of animals, birds, reptiles and creatures of the sea have been tamed by man, but no man can tame the tongue. It is a restless evil full of deadly poison. With the same tongue we praise the Lord and with it we curse men who have come from G's likeness. Out of the same mouth come praise and cursing." Maybe that is why the snake's tongue is forked. There is an analogy here somewhere, I'm sure.

Notice how the snake employed the most common deception still played on humans to date. His first words were "Did G really say …?" The question is intended not to encourage the woman to make a power play but rather to plant the seed of doubt.

> The woman said to the serpent, "We may eat fruit from the trees in the garden, but G did say, 'You must not eat fruit from the tree that is in the middle of the garden, and you must not touch it, or you will die.'"

This moment will eventually serve as the basis for significant misguided persecution against women. The woman talks to the snake. Before you rush to indict the woman, remember she wasn't created when G proclaimed the prohibition. In fact, what she tells the serpent isn't even identical to what G told Adam. She got inconsistent information from somewhere.

Regardless of her lack of actual knowledge, she did know something was up with the tree. She had constructive knowledge. The woman is not without blame; she knew better. Sometimes humans

---

[50] Genesis doesn't specifically state that the serpent is Lucifer but the snake's argument of wanting to be like the Most High mirrors the accusation made against Lucifer in the book of Isaiah. Interesting to note, Lucifer, not the woman, was the first to be deceived. Lucifer deceived himself into believing he was or could ever be equal to G.

may not know what G specifically prohibits, but they still have a sinking suspicion that something is wrong. Just because you didn't hear from G directly—or simply failed to follow up with G about what is and is not acceptable—doesn't make something allowable. All humans are responsible for seeking understanding and wisdom for themselves and not relying on the hearsay of others. The woman's mistake, like many humans after her, was not seeking out the will or the word of G. Ignorance is not a defense.

> "You will not surely die," the serpent said to the woman. "For G knows that when you eat of it your eyes will be opened, and you will be like G, knowing good and evil." When the woman saw that the fruit of the tree was good for food and pleasing to the eye, and also desirable for gaining wisdom, she took some and ate it.

The critical thing to notice here is that nothing happens. The woman ate and nothing happened. The lack of "falling" can serve different purposes. Some see the fact that nothing happens as reinforcement of the fact that G never told the woman to avoid the fruit. Others believe that the pause highlights that awkward, misleading lull that frequently lingers between a sin and its consequence. Regardless, the woman had some idea that the fruit was a no-no; so there was some less-than-honorable motivation in the eating. Deciding to partake of a taboo activity is generally an act reserved for the rebellious or teenagers ... perhaps that last part is redundant.

Most sins, though, do not have immediate consequences, thereby making them appear rather harmless. The quiet calm before the storm can mask the connection between the sin and the consequence. Absent a direct and immediate effect, you humans are often encouraged to keep indulging in the bad acts. Once the consequences catch up, the bottom drops out. You humans kill me with your shock and surprise at the turmoil you unleash inside yourselves.

Notice how the woman begins with a logical argument as to why she should take the fruit. "It is good for food." So are all the other fruits and vegetables, but she undercuts the regulation by taking what she knows is wrong and grouping it with what is allowed. This is the first step to letting the sin take hold. Put everything in the world into one pot, and then nothing is wrong or bad. Let's just throw the roast beef, ice cream, and crickets into one large pot to make a giant stew of absolutes. They can all be eaten, so let's not discriminate. Everything can be done, so let's not limit ourselves.

No boundaries. That's a huge problem. As long as you can keep boundaries between the wrong and the right, the scope creep won't happen … and remember, G gave you power over creeps. Once you group all behaviors into one pool, you diminish morality. It's like mixing dessert in with the main course—it ruins the meal. Yeah, I know, the food is all going to the same place, but the essence of dinner is lost if it is blended with dessert. They are separate for a reason.

The sacred and profane need to be kept separate, not because there isn't gray, but because when you start falling down that slippery slope, you lose self-discipline. Once a human blurs boundaries, self-control is an illusion.

If you were to legalize drugs, theft, trespass, assault, and murder, you would eliminate crime because nothing would be illegal. If you eliminate all laws and rules, no one could ever commit a crime. Of course, humans will be reduced to pure animal behavior, and there would be no security or morality. A society without morality would forego all self-control.

Before she ever actually ate the fruit, the woman bore fruit of the Tree of the Knowledge of Good Evil. She provided opening arguments for her own personal benefit. She didn't consider the greater good, the relationship with G, the impact on the man, or the consequences. She made a decision based solely on a selfish rationale. It was "good," "pleasing," and "desirable" to her and *her alone*. She was proud and Pride is the fruit of the Tree of the Knowledge of Good and Evil.

> She also gave some to her husband, who was with her, and he ate it. Then the eyes of both of them were opened, and they realized they were naked; so they sewed fig leaves together and made coverings for themselves.

Ah! Now the man eats. Now the fall[51] occurs! It wasn't until after *the man* ate the forbidden food that their eyes were opened. You could argue that woman fell *because* the man ate. Remember, it was said that the "two of them shall become one." Those words were quite akin to a wedding vow. A vow to G is quite serious. If it was vowed that they were one, then man's fall would bring woman down with him.[52]

Notwithstanding, who was really exercising authority here? No one was listening to G, that part is clear. The woman gave the fruit to the man and he ate—despite everything he knew to be right and to the contrary. That the man followed the woman's lead suggests that authority was resting with her. She didn't hold him down, bat her eyes, or otherwise force the fruit down his throat. She offered; he ate. The man and the woman weren't necessarily ignoring G. They weren't trying to be completely rebellious. But they focused only on themselves. The relationship with G was pushed into the background.

Their pride allowed them to rationalize their behavior. And after the escalation of pride kicks in, there is a fall. Escalations are quite annoying that way. They lift you up higher just so the grounded reality will be that much farther away and hurt that much more when you hit. G made humans out of dust, not air. G made humans grounded. Humans spend their days increasing an illusory worth. You get great titles, letters behind your name, brand-name clothes, fancy cars, posh trinkets, and houses so big they cram the outside world together. What people don't get is the balance in the spiritual and the physical. You can't keep from the world *and* give to it at the same time. When you spend your time increasing your worldly position, you take from your spiritual position. You draw on the reserve of the spiritual offerings until you become spiritually bankrupt.

You know, there will be generations of people to come who will point the finger at this man and woman and accusingly cry out about

---

[51] Once their eyes were opened and they realized they were naked, they had to take the leaves from the trees to hide. I think that is why the season when the leaves come off is called fall.

[52] Much like the concept of joint and several liability.

the evil that has entered the world through Eve and Adam. But the story isn't about woman allegedly tempting man. It isn't about man bringing woman down. G isn't telling you this story so you can sit in judgment of other people and find how to assess blame. In fact, if you are spending a great deal of time trying to determine which party was more culpable, then you are actually committing the sin that man and woman committed.

It is all about admitting your personal culpability. G is hoping you learn from the mistakes of Adam and Eve. Everyone has a garden. Each and every human begins like Adam. They all begin in communion with G. They all are given a world where they can choose to benefit others or to benefit only themselves. Humans can choose to see the good in everything or the bad. They choose to build people up or break them down. Every time a human chooses the bad, it is not because they were tempted, victimized, or oppressed. It is because they made the choice. Just because a choice was made easy, doesn't mean it is right. It isn't Adam's fault there is sin in your world. It isn't the fault of the entire gender of women or the fault of snakes. It's your choice.

> Then the man and his wife heard the sound of G as G was walking in the garden in the cool of the day, and they hid from G among the trees of the garden. But G called to the man, "Where are you?"

G's sense of humor is so often missed in Scripture. People forget that G isn't "here" or "there." Scripture is filled with examples in which someone tried to hide from G, yet G is always there and here and everywhere. David[53] figures this out. He correctly mentions in a psalm that there is nowhere he can go where G is not. G resides in heaven, and Luke correctly points out that the kingdom of heaven is *within* you. G is an integral part of man. Sure, G may play an advanced form of peek-a-boo in which the hands cover the face and then open up when you least expect it, but G is always there. For man

---

[53] David comes in a later story and is known for his love for G, dancing naked, and taking Goliath to his first rock concert. He is found in the books of Samuel, Psalms (silent P) and a little in Kings (loud K).

to hide from G is rather silly and further evidence that man does not know with whom he is dealing. G doesn't move. G is everywhere. It was man that moved; G points that out: "Where are you?"—because you aren't with me.

The fundamental premise in any cross-examination is to never ask a question to which you do not already know the answer. Similarly, G's questions aren't for the benefit of the "askor," they are for the benefit of the "askee." G doesn't cross-examine, per se, but G does want to give everyone the opportunity to perform the standard rite of forgiveness,[54] accuse, or deny everything—whatever the soul cries out over that slippery serpent of a tongue. G states that out of the mouth, the heart speaks. You can find out what people are harboring by letting them talk long enough. Still, the response is for the benefit of the man. Will he take the opportunity to think about what he did? Why did he do what he did? With whom did he do it? This last point isn't as critical, but I like to say the word *whom* every now and then. I can't always get chronology down pat, so I have to demonstrate some form of higher education.

What parent hasn't asked his or her child who is standing before a well-colored wall, "What are you doing?" Why do parents ask such things? They ask because the response of the child is important in determining how to deal with the situation. If the child says, "I wanted to make you a beautiful picture," it is bound to get a different reaction than if the child says, "What does it look like I am doing? Duh! You should have bought me more paper!" G knew *what* the man and woman had done but was more interested in *why* they had done it and whether they even cared about what they had just done. G sticks with relationship-building. There was no judgment as to why the man did what he did. In fact, after the one and only rule was broken, G still let the man and woman tell their stories. G gave them a chance. They blew it.

> He answered, "I heard you in the garden, and I was afraid because I was naked; so I hid."

---

[54] Think, Repent, Repeat. (Repeat the process of thinking and repenting, not sinning.)

The man's response demonstrates that he simply did not know G. Had he truly known G, he would have known what thousands of others have quickly figured out: G is everywhere, and you will always lose if you try to play a game of hide-and-seek with G. Tag is a little tough too.

There is another story in Scripture in which the leading actor simply didn't understand. I'm not talking about Jonah, although he exhibited similar tendencies as Adam. I'm talking about the story of the prodigal son. I'm sure you know the story, but since I enjoy it so much, I'll recount a bit of it. Well, I'll recount Jesus' story as told by Luke.[55]

> There was a man who had two sons. The younger one said to his father, "Father, give me my share of the estate." So he divided his property between them. Not long after that, the younger son got together all he had, set off for a distant country and there squandered his wealth in wild living. After he had spent everything, there was a severe famine in that whole country, and he began to be in need. So he went and hired himself out to a citizen of that country, who sent him to his fields to feed pigs. He longed to fill his stomach with the pods that the pigs were eating, but no one gave him anything.
>
> When he came to his senses, he said, "How many of my father's hired men have food to spare, and here I am starving to death! I will set out and go back to my father and say to him: 'Father, I have sinned against heaven and against you. I am no longer worthy to be called your son; make me like one of your hired men.'" So he got up and went to his father.
>
> But while he was still a long way off, his father saw him and was filled with compassion for him; he ran to his son, threw his arms around him and kissed him. The son said to him, "Father, I have sinned against heaven and against you. I am no longer worthy to be called your son."
>
> But the father said to his servants, "Quick! Bring the best robe and put it on him. Put a ring on his finger and sandals on his feet. Bring the fattened calf and kill it. Let's have a feast and celebrate. For this son of mine was dead and is alive again; he was lost and is found." So they began to celebrate.

---

[55] Author of one of the four Gospels. No relation to Darth Vader.

Meanwhile, the older son was in the field. When he came near the house, he heard music and dancing. So he called one of the servants and asked him what was going on. "Your brother has come," he replied, "and your father has killed the fattened calf because he has him back safe and sound."

The older brother became angry and refused to go in. So his father went out and pleaded with him. But he answered his father, "Look! All these years I've been slaving for you and never disobeyed your orders. Yet you never gave me even a young goat so I could celebrate with my friends. But when this son of yours who has squandered your property with prostitutes comes home, you kill the fattened calf for him!"

"My son," the father said, "you are always with me, and everything I have is yours. But we had to celebrate and be glad, because this brother of yours was dead and is alive again; he was lost and is found."

The best thing about this story is that you humans always seem to jump to the conclusion that the son who left and returned after a life a debauchery is the prodigal son. But really, he's just the easier one to target. It's like that age-old question, who is buried in Grant's tomb? Sure, it's easy to yell, "Grant!" but his wife is also there. And actually, since it's an above-ground vault, no one is actually buried. There is more to the question than meets the eye; you'll *grant* me that, ha-ha.

Who acted irresponsibly? The behavior of both sons indicates naiveté about their father. One son assumed his father would refuse his repentant heart and force him into a substandard position. The other son assumed his dad would reward him for following all the rules. Notice this "good son" states he "never disobeyed" his father's orders. Maybe he didn't, but he didn't run to embrace his long-lost brother either. In fact, he was jealous. No hugging, no welcome back, no "Do you want your old room back?" from him. The "good son" thought he was entitled to more. At least the returning son recognized his failing and sought forgiveness. You never hear about love, repentance, or forgiveness from the older brother.

Humans do the same. They often fail to turn to G for fear they will be judged and punished; or, alternatively, they follow strict rules, neglect compassion, and then demand compensation. G's rules teach you how to separate the good from the bad or the holy from the profane so you can more easily avoid that creepy slope or the slippery-scope creep. But it is *love* for G and for others that will keep you on firm ground.

The father demonstrated pure love. He did not favor either son but simply loved the different sons completely.

> And G said, "Who told you that you were naked? Have you eaten from the tree that I commanded you not to eat from?"

You can almost hear the theme song from *Jeopardy* resonating in the garden. Small woodland creatures stop with inquisitive poses waiting to hear what man will utter next. The beavers are placing bets in the background. Everyone knows what has happened and what is happening—everyone except the man. G goes directly to man and points out that it was man who was told not to eat from the tree. Since man was directly told by G, man is held directly accountable for his violation.

Some people argue that G went to man because he was in charge, but no such hierarchy had yet been established. To the contrary, only G ruled over the humans at this point in time. Man had no power over woman at all. This is evidenced by four points. 1) Man followed woman's lead in the fruit eating endeavor. 2) G will, in later dialogue, grant to the man actual authority, *which means it wasn't there initially.* 3) Adam couldn't name the woman until after the fall; and 4) it was well accepted that women exercised significant influence over men. A good man can fall into a wayward life if married to a woman of questionable character. But a man of questionable character can become good with a pious wife. The fact that a woman possesses the ability to influence a man should come as no surprise; she is a "helper." G created her for that purpose. She is not a "tempter." She influences, not tempts because a man can go down either a sacred or a profane path based on the wife he chooses and the choices he makes. The Book of Peter states that men who do not believe the Word can be won over by the behavior of their wives. A woman can point a man away or toward G. Ultimately though, the man is responsible his own decisions.

Well, this is the moment to shine, the point where man can truly think about what he did, the moment where man can be the returning prodigal son. He was separated from G by pride but could be restored through humility. Man failed to recognize that the problem was not the fruit, the woman, the snake, or G. It was his sin. G teed up the relationship, pointed man toward the green, and gave him a great set of clubs. Man whiffed. He lifted his head and shifted his focus.

> The man said, "The woman you put here with me—she gave me some fruit from the tree, and I ate it."

Way to go, big guy. Like the old saying goes, "There is no greater sacrifice than someone else." He threw the woman under the bus faster than you can say "apple turnover." Man was getting legal on G. He found a loophole! *I didn't eat from the tree; the woman gave it to me. I ate the fruit from the woman!* Technicalities don't really work with G. Man took no responsibility for his part in the bad act; again, evidence that the man didn't know G. You would be hard-pressed to have a deep relationship with G and still be willing to deny accountability.

Important distinction to note here: not only did Adam accuse the woman, he also directly accused G: "*You* put her here with me." The Bible speaks of how children are cursed by the sins of their parents. It isn't that G forces the child into some punishment; it is just that parents can blur morality and, therefore, lead their children astray by parental bad acts. If parents sin but try to justify it to their children, the children may not categorize those actions as bad. Having trusted their parents to define right and wrong, the children may be quicker to adopt the behavior at issue and, therefore, bring about consequences on their own heads.

Think of it this way, imagine you had a bottle of poison in your home and you put a brightly colored label on the bottle that said "Poison." You add a skull and crossbones to the bottle and avoid it like the plague. If, in some moment of weakness, you indulge—you get help for what you have done. You warn your kids about it. You tell your kids how you were made weaker by the poison.

Now, pretend you have that same bottle of poison but you don't label it at all or, worse yet, you call it "candy." The same bottle of poison is now exponentially more dangerous because your children can't see the harm.

Sin is the same way. If you call it by a fluffy name, deny that it is dangerous or casually indulge, you discount the harm. This is why there should come a time in every person's life when they no longer rely solely on any other person—such as their parents—for standards of morality. All people should seek their own salvation through relationship with G. Relying on the interpretation of fallible people can lead other fallible people down a dangerous path.

It is very important to admit your sin, not only as a sign of contrition but also to help keep the lines clear between the sacred and profane. If you herald, like the good son did, that you have followed every rule and done nothing that would require an apology; then let me be the first to proclaim that G has sent only one Messiah ... and you are not it.[56]

> Then the LORD G said to the woman, "What is this you have done?"
> The woman said, "The serpent deceived me, and I ate."

Again, upon confrontation of the sin there is no repentance, no accountability, no admission – only blame. G realized that the man wasn't going to obtain any enlightenment any time soon. G shifted the questioning to the woman. G doesn't ask the man about the woman's actions. The man does not speak for her, nor was he responsible for her. G held her accountable for her own actions, but notice that G does not make any reference to the command. I'm just saying....

Here we go again. How many times have you done something you knew was patently wrong, but it was just so much easier to

---

[56] If, after reading that paragraph, you still believe you are perfect, then the only remaining cure for you would be to get married. You will quickly learn your shortcomings.

justify it by heralding someone else's shortcomings? He ignores me, she doesn't satisfy me, I had a bad day, my boss had it coming, or the devil made me do it. This last one is funny. Humans can come up with far worse things than the devil himself concocts. Don't get me wrong—the devil loves to tempt. After all, misery loves company. But once you suppress that whispering voice of G, humans can come up with some crazy things. The devil learns more from mortal musings than he devises on his own.

Adam broke the *letter* of the law; the-woman broke the *spirit* of the law. They both sinned. Humans continue with these two lines of offense, and there are consequences to both. There are those people who have the Word of G and know what they are supposed to do but fail to do it. There are others who may not have the actual Word but still know that an act is wrong when they commit it. Adam received express direction from G and failed to obey. The woman failed to find out specifically what G required. She didn't seek the personal relationship with G. She let someone else tell her what G wanted.

> So the LORD G said to the serpent, "Because you have done this, Cursed are you above all the livestock and all the wild animals! You will crawl on your belly and you will eat dust all the days of your life. And I will put enmity between you and the woman, and between your offspring and hers; he will crush your head, and you will strike his heel."

We all get that the serpent is symbolic of evil, the devil, the medical profession—Oh! Sidebar for a moment. If you happen to peruse the Old Testament, you will read about a time when the Israelites wouldn't stop complaining. G delivered them from slavery, gave them food and water, but they were just like those annoying coworkers who complain no matter what the situation—it's too hot, it's too cold, the water cooler's broken, the doughnuts are stale, on and on and on … with no off. Every time they, —the Israelites, not the coworkers—asked for something, G provided. Yet the Israelites couldn't seem to figure out the one goal G has for mankind—to be happy doing good.⁵⁷ You can't just be happy and do nothing, nor should you be grumpy about doing good. Anyway, G finally said—and did—that one thing most parents have threatened their children with at least once in their lives: "If you are going to keep crying, I'll give you something to cry about."

G sent snakes among the people. If a complainer got bitten, he or she died. Now those other issues didn't seem so important. Now they had something real to cry about. The Israelites turned back to G and requested help. G had Moses craft a bronze snake and put it on a stick. If anyone was bitten by a snake, he or she simply had to look upon the snake-on-a-stick, and they would be healed. It was the power of G that would heal them, but G respected the people's need for something tangible. Hence, the snake.

Well, eventually the people forgot that the healing came from G, and they began to worship the snake-on-a-stick⁵⁸ independently of G. The snake became an idol. Hezekiah, a guy that came a few generations after Moses, destroyed the snake because the people had misaligned their faith.⁵⁹

Scripture will prophesy that the Son of Man will be lifted up like this snake. The Messiah will be affixed to a stick and set out for display. Any who would look upon him in faith would be saved. Any crucifix supports this long-standing belief. Of course, it is not the crucifix itself that has healing powers but the faith in the source of the healing—G.

Since I am talking about the healing powers of sticks, I would be remiss in my contextual obligations if I left out the waters of Marah. When the Israelites came out of the Red Sea and were formally freed of the oppression of Pharaoh, they wandered for three days. They got

---

[57] Wise Solomon reiterates this point in Ecclesiastes. In fact, he went so far as to state that everything else is done in vain.

[58] Often confused with a state-fair delicacy.

[59] Well, today's medical world is often represented by two snakes-on-a-stick. (It's the new and improved snake-on-a-stick.) The emblem and the healers associated with it serve as a great reminder of G's healing ability, but it is still critical to remember that the ultimate source of the healing is not the emblem or the healers but G working through the healers.

thirsty. They came to the waters of Marah, which was bitter water. The people became to grumble. Funny enough, they grumbled to Moses instead of simply asking the G who had just delivered them. See, G just did a very amazing feat by splitting the sea in two, letting the Israelites pass, and swallowing up their pursuers. The Israelites knew G could handle the issues they were facing, but instead of calling to G and asking for help, they decided to complain to someone else. Humans do this all the time. Instead of going directly to the source with a problem, they like to vent and rant to various other people, resulting in negative attitudes that spread like poison.

If I pour a little bitter water into a bucket of sweet water, I will contaminate the whole thing. One angry outlook can corrupt so many healthy perspectives. This is why it is important to prune yourself and make sure you aren't introducing poison into your words, thoughts, and actions.

Humans must let go of the bitterness. It doesn't matter how many wonderful gifts you are given; if you have bitterness in your heart, you will be ungrateful. Without gratitude you can't find grace.

Moses corrected the bitterness of the water by throwing a stick of wood into the water. This wood, commonly associated with the wood of the cross, was able to remove the bitterness. It is through the cross that a human can learn to let go of the anger inside. It is a critical first step to becoming grateful and quenching that spiritual thirst.

Interestingly enough, the word *marah* means bitter, but not in a purely bad sense. The Hebrew origin of the word also carries with it a connotation of strength. On a simple level, bitter herbs are also known as strong herbs. On a deeper level, when Naomi[60] calls herself Marah after her husband and sons have died—she isn't succumbing or giving in to the tragedy that has befallen her. She is claiming to be made stronger through the grief.

Back to the main discussion. I am so bad about chronology! The "he" in the Genesis passage refers to the one who will ultimately defeat what snakes bring—death. The "he" is the Messiah. Sure the snake will lash out at the Messiah and strike his heel, but a nip at the

---

[60] Naomi's story is found in the book of Ruth; a lovely story in which the mother-in-law and daughter-in-law actually got along quite well.

heel means nothing when your own head is crushed. I'd take a good heel-nipping over a head-crushing any day! It is interesting to note that when a person is crucified, the heel can become torn up as it is pressed against the wood in feeble attempts to lift the body in order to breathe. Jesus had a pretty damaged heel from his stint on the cross. However, it is this sore-heeled Messiah who will ultimately crush the head of death.

Death is a fascinating subject. Humans can go all sorts of places on this subject. Did you know that when people are dying, their breathing pattern resembles that of mother giving birth? Also, a dying person tends to take on the sleeping pattern of a newborn. They sleep at sporadic times on and off throughout the day.

These similarities are subtle reminders from G that death is merely the birth into a new world. You can imagine that there comes a time in the lives of fetuses when they wish the womb was larger. They get cramped; it's hard to move. They hear the faint echo of a mother's voice rumbling through their existence. At some point, when the contractions start, the fetus wishes for more room, for the discomfort to stop, for womb service. Babies have no idea what is in store for them. While labor may be scary, uncomfortable, loud, bright, confusing, and even painful, there is a point when the baby realizes that the loss of the only world it had ever known pales in comparison to where it has arrived. Before the baby may have suspected there was a larger being that loved it, but it couldn't be sure. It couldn't see its mother. It could only see right in front of its face. Sometimes, on a quiet night, it could hear a distant whisper but it didn't understand the words. After the transition, the baby meets its parent face to face. That distant voice is now very real and the warm arms that embrace the child help it to learn that the words it heard earlier were sung out of love.

Death is just that—rebirth into something far grander than your current mind can conceive. If fetuses could debate, they would probably argue that there is nothing beyond what they see, hear, or taste while they are in the womb. By the time they learn otherwise, they are unable to go back to tell the others. Voyages like birth tend to be one-way trips, and besides, fetuses tend to keep these things quiet.[61]

Equating this life with being in heavenly utero also explains why it is harmful to take a life before its time. When the baby is ready to be born, it will be. Taking it too soon before its due date causes damage to the baby and the mother and can devastate the expectant parents and siblings. When people are ready to leave this life, they will go. Taking them too soon hurts too many. Saying that what happens to your life should not affect the lives of others is equivalent to saying you have the right to crash your side of the airplane. Lives are too interconnected to suggest that the choice of one person will not hurt anyone else.

But death is also not to be feared. I like to think of it as a massive change of scenery. Perhaps you have gone fishing before. Maybe you have caught a fish, brought him into the boat and then thrown him back into the water. Did you ever wonder what that fish thought or if the other fish believed his story of the weird, topsy-turvy world? Maybe prose will help as I have found that things are easier to understand when they rhyme.

> The angels in heaven love to play games
> For they are fond fishers of men.
> They bait their hooks with small bits of glory
> To see what worthy catch to bring in.
>
> Men bide their days with baited brilliance abound
> Often not giving a good look.
> Until they see clearly the beauty before them
> And eagerly jump on the hook.
>
> Sometimes … the angels reel slowly
> Ensuring the hook has been set.
> Sometimes the angels reel quickly
> And swiftly scoop with their nets.

---

[61] One of the few things about which they are quiet!

> There should be no fear when you're caught in the snare,
> Only compassion and hope.
> For there is only love, forgiveness, and grace
> In G's most heavenly boat.

There is a distinction with death that I should make. Death is a consequence for sin. However, I will explain later, in the section about the Tree of Life, that death as a consequence can be defeated. When death is defeated, the loss of the body merely becomes a relocation of the spirit. Death is shifting from the mortal to the immortal. But I'm getting ahead of myself. Back to the snake. Keep in mind that G *cursed* the serpent. G does not curse the humans. The man and the woman don't share in the *punishment* of the tempter. G simply gives them what they asked for.

> To the woman G said, "I will greatly increase your pains in childbearing; with pain you will give birth to children. Your desire will be for your husband, and he will rule over you." To Adam G said, "Because you listened to your wife and ate from the tree about which I commanded you, 'You must not eat of it,' cursed is the ground because of you; through painful toil you will eat of it all the days of your life. It will produce thorns and thistles for you and you will eat the plants of the field. By the sweat of your brow you will eat your food until you return to the ground, since from it you were taken; for dust you are and to dust you will return."

Many people think G was punishing man and woman here. To the contrary, G is giving them exactly what they asked for. It wasn't a punishment at all. It was a consequence. The woman could already have children, a necessity since G said to multiply. The man already had to work the garden, remember? But these things were good. The humans wanted to know good *and* bad.[62]

Pre-fall, women had children, and this was good. Now she has pain with childbirth, and this is bad. The man previously worked the

---

[62] Pretty bad bill of goods, eh? The Tree had the knowledge of good and bad but they already knew good. In essence, they were eating to get the knowledge of bad. It was all in the marketing.

garden, and this was good. Now he has to work really hard—"toil" and this is bad. It is like the teenager who so eagerly wants his own car as opposed to borrowing yours. Sure, the car is freedom and fun. Oh, but then there are the car payments, insurance payments, and the costs of gas and maintenance. The good has a downside. Before, G was letting them drive the car with no strings attached. Then humans wanted complete autonomy, and they got it. Now G handed over the invoices to cover the costs of the car. Humans learned the price of the lessening of their knowledge of good. They learned bad.

It's funny when you think about it. Women tend to be more the caretakers of the children, and the women suffer the most in bringing the children forth. Men tend to be more likely to focus on their jobs, and it is this work that will cause them to suffer. The source of their happiness requires labor. The things humans get without any effort at all are rarely appreciated as much.

Another result from this fruit-eating binge is that G told the woman her desire will be for her husband, who will rule over her. Think about it. This was a noted *change*. If woman desired the man to begin with, G wouldn't have had to call this out as a change. Try to imagine woman's reaction when G pretty much said, "Oh, and now, you are going to want *him*."

What you had before the fall was a man who was so gaga over the woman that he vowed in front of G that they "would be one." Imagine many a guy, presented with such specimen of beauty, wiping drool from his face and pretty much agreeing to pull any stupid stunt to win her attention[63] and perhaps hoping for a chance to be a factor in the multiplication equation. You knew Adam wanted the woman. He was alone without her. He was happy with her. It was "not good" when he was without her. It was "very good" when he was with her. He followed her lead at snack time.

Before the fall, you had a woman who could take or leave the whole man thing. She didn't say she liked him, wanted him, or even noticed him. Up until now, all you know of the woman's feelings about man is indifference. What *is* evident by the woman's actions is that the woman had exercised significant independence from

---

[63] Like eating taboo fruit.

the man. She didn't consult Adam before snacking on the fruit. He followed *her* lead.

A husband and wife cannot be one if half the team really doesn't care about the other half, whether emotionally or logically. Man already desired woman. So what did G do? G made woman desire the man. G leveled the playing field.

Next, G said man would rule over woman. Man already submitted to woman and forgot about his obligation to G. So what did G do? G made man have authority over woman. Again, G leveled the playing field.

The desire and the authority had to go together. If G mandated only that woman had desire of man but she maintained complete authority over the man, the man might easily become an object to be abused. Women would be making men perform all sorts of tricks and games in order to obtain their affection or math skills. Conversely, if the man had *authority* but left off the fact that the woman would desire the man, then odds are very few women would ever marry, else they simply sign up to a life of servitude. Now there was equality.

G instilled balance where there was none. Man desired woman; woman had apparent authority over man. To balance this reality, G made woman desire man and gave man authority.

Oddly enough, this passage, intended to prevent objectifying humans, was wielded as authority to do just that to women. For centuries, men seized on the "authority" as permission to dominate and control women.

First of all, the goal in granting actual authority to men was to establish balance, synergy, and to cultivate the primary relationship which was with G. Second, authority does not equate with supremacy. G provided the model for authority. G ruled over all humans and expected that same means of ruling to be exercised when bestowing actual authority on man and even with apparent authority in women. The Book of Exodus proclaims the attributes of G.[64] These are expected to be emulated by people in authority. These attributes include being compassionate, gracious, slow to anger, faithful, forgiving wickedness, and abounding in and maintaining

---

[64] See Exodus 34.

love. G has always sought the greatest good. G has always loved completely. This is expected of those in authority.

Paul, that prolific 'postle' with a penchant for proper point-making, stated in his letter to the Ephesians that a husband is to love his wife just as Christ loved the church. He is to keep her holy and blameless (can't keep finding faults), and he is to love his wife as much as he loves himself. If a man would do something to his wife that he would not do to himself, he doesn't get it. If a man cares more for building his body, his career, and his ambitions than building up his wife—He doesn't get it.[65]

I should comment on the "Dust you shall return" bit. In olden, future days, scholars believed that G made people with a spirit and a body because G knew they would sin. If they were bad and had a spirit, they would live forever in Paradise; well then, there goes the neighborhood. If they were good and had only bodies, they couldn't enjoy future bliss. By giving them both, those who pursued only the things of the earth would die and become part of it. Those with noble, spiritual pursuits would find the eternal paradise that they seek.

> Adam named his wife Eve, because she would become the mother of all the living.

Funny, Eve didn't even have a name up until this point. Naming was a pretty significant action. To name something suggested dominion over it. Prior to the fruit munching, Adam didn't have dominion over her, nor could he. G made him a "helper," a translation of the original word would be *counterpart*. Think of the suspension on a vehicle. The left side of the vehicle's suspension is identical to the right, yet they are different in that they cannot simply be interchanged. Neither is superior nor inferior, and both must function as designed in order to move the greater vehicle forward. One is not better than the other, but they are different. *Vive la différence!* Now that man had authority, he could formally name the woman. Good thing he wasn't feeling spiteful or angry when he picked her name.

---

[65] This statement works on many levels.

The LORD G made garments of skin for Adam and his wife and clothed them.

This is what put fear into the animals. It only takes one animal sacrifice to cause the other animals to know that humans can be trouble. From this time forward, animals fear man. And if they didn't, they didn't stick around much longer anyway. The animals took a vote as to which of them should be sacrificed. The vote was pretty much unanimous—the snake. While the snake was the most logical choice, it was actually a Lamb that was slain at creation.[66]

Something else that most people don't realize is that once one person sins, it does affect everyone. You can't shoot a hole in your end of the boat and not expect the other riders to get miffed. Think about it. You live in a happy, pleasant community. The houses are always unlocked. Children run up and down the streets even past dark. Keys are left in cars. Bicycles lay in the front yards. Then you hear a criminal is in the area. All of a sudden, your behavior changes. The doors get locked. The children stay close. You have to wear clothes now. Well, the people in the garden did. One bad apple spoiled it for the whole lot.

Now people wonder whom they can trust. If Adam and Eve could sin, perhaps others could too. Why didn't they see it coming? They were such a nice couple. What was it about those two that made them sin? Was it the area of the garden they lived in? Was it the way they looked? How could people proactively identify other potential offenders? There had to be an easier way to identify sinners than actually getting to know people. Humans were reluctant to build relationships with other people who possess the capability of sin. They needed a quick fix, an alternative to relationships, so they wouldn't waste their time with people who might hurt them. The fear birthed judgment and stereotypes. It is a blessing that you can't tell what sins other people may commit lest you humans become

---

[66] See the book of Revelation for more on this revelation. John's reference to the "Lamb" doesn't mean that Christ was killed twice but that his death and subsequent salvation of humans were planned during the first 6 days—creation. Since G is not subject to time, the fact that Jesus' death and resurrection were ordained during creation should not be a surprise.

even more judgmental and fully exclude those who need the love of society. Ostracizing a repentant sinner only breeds evil.

All humans are sinners. Yet, sometimes humans get comfortable with their *own* sins and seek harm against others that commit different offenses. Scared humans wish that sinners wore physical badges proclaiming their weaknesses.[67] That way you could tell what sins a human could commit by looking at him or her and then appropriately condemn them. People could generate a false sense of security based on superficial stereotypes.

Humans continue to perpetrate sin through stereotyping. Humanity should be greatly ashamed of some its actions throughout history, er, the future. People found it easier to create fears and myths about people of certain colors, religions, genders, preferences. Humans felt empowered by sitting back and lumping entire populations into giant generalizations. It is so much easier simply to assign blame for the world's ills to certain people because of completely benign traits. The judges had to pick the big and obvious traits too, because the traits that *really* are attributable to the world's ills require far too much effort to see or correct. Truth be told, judging is simply illusory protection and is the recourse for the socially and spiritually lazy. Instead of reaching out and learning about people, it became easier to stay back at a distance and interact only with those select few who met superficial prerequisites. Problem is, once you start judging people, you have no time to love them. I'd love to take credit for that last line, but Mother Teresa said it before me ... well, she will say it before me.

> And G said, "The man has now become like one of us, knowing good and evil. He must not be allowed to reach out his hand and take also from the Tree of Life and eat, and live forever."

The Tree of the Knowledge of Good and Evil is easy to comprehend. It's so easy, even a snake can figure it out. It is learning and striving for one's own *personal* benefit. It is growing and cultivating

---

[67] Forgetting that they, themselves, would have to pronounce to the world their darker side.

pride. The Tree of Life is a bit more complicated. I would tell you to put that on the back burner, but it is going to be a while before I get to it, so you might just want to put it in the fridge so we can prepare it later.

> So the Lord G banished him from the garden of Eden to work the ground from which he had been taken. After G drove the man out, G placed on the east side of the garden of Eden cherubim and a flaming sword flashing back and forth to guard the way to the Tree of Life."

First, you have to wonder what the sword represents. Ideally, I would be telling you about the Tree of Life first, but that topic is a bit more in-depth and will come later.[68] The sword is, however, that weapon wielded by the Messiah—the manifestation of the Word of G. The sword is the tool, the portion of the Word of G, which separates the *actions* from the *heart* of man. It pierces to the very soul and can even discern the thoughts and intents of the heart.[69] Don't think that you can casually walk to the Tree of Life. Your actions will not gain you eternal life; before you can taste of the Tree, your very heart must be transformed.

The Messiah seeks to put peace in each person's heart because it is the very heart of man that will be judged. Messiah cannot bring peace to the earth as a whole because it is the *choice* of each person; but Messiah can bring peace to each person, if they choose. This is why Jesus criticized the Pharisees. They did all the right actions for all the wrong reasons. Paul says, "And if I give all my possessions to feed the poor, and I surrender my body to be burned, but do not have love, it profits me nothing … But now faith, hope, love, abide these three; but the greatest of these is love."[70]

---

[68] You can probably take this point out of the fridge now and let it thaw.

[69] Hebrews 4 supports this affirmation. Also, Isaiah 49; Ephesians 6; Revelation 1; and Revelation 2.

[70] Feel free to review 1 Corinthians 13 for more insight on this or attend almost any wedding to get the complete reading.

You can't trick G. You can't buy your way into eternal bliss by going through the motions. It is not your motions that will be judged. It is your very heart. Of course, if you truly cultivate love within yourself, those works will follow. You can't love and be apathetic at the same time.

Many humans wonder why being transformed doesn't equate to material wealth or prosperity. They feel slighted when bad things happen to good people or when good things happen to bad people. They think that because they are saved, the troubles of the world should escape them. Even the prophet Habakkuk cried out to G with similar time-honored questions.[71]

Habakkuk's first complaint is, *Why does G tolerate wrong?* He feels that the law is "paralyzed" and justice doesn't prevail. G is good, so why would G let bad run rampant? G replies to the complaint by reminding Habakkuk that he has no idea what G is doing. Sure, bad guys raise armies, but they don't defeat G. But when G raises an army—who will save the evil ones? Bad guys may win battles; G wins wars. Wicked people's only god is themselves—or their own strength. That answer is extremely profound when you consider that if fallible people have only themselves as salvation, their rescue will be short-lived.

Habakkuk's second complaint is that bad people get lots of money and power while many believers have little money or power. G responds with the equivalent of "Yep. There are wicked who have money and power and choice food and drink. *But you have the Almighty G.*" Sure, bad people have lots of worldly things, but what does it matter to the person who has a relationship with the Divine? Once you know G, the things of this world are of little importance, and they will not save you when true disaster nears. Why would anybody care what other people have if they were in relationship with the Holy One? When you have G, you have more than the world can offer. Find comfort in that relationship, not the things of the world.

---

[71] His book is short, so it's an easy read. And the name is funny to say.

Act 4: Genesis 4, Cain and Abel

Adam lay with his wife Eve, and she became pregnant and gave birth to Cain. She said, "With the help of the LORD I have brought forth a man." Later she gave birth to his brother Abel. Now Abel kept flocks, and Cain worked the soil.

Isn't it weird how many shepherds the Bible brings up? Shepherding—good shepherding—requires a great deal of patience, compassion, and strength. And deodorant. Many central, reverent biblical figures were shepherds—Abel, Moses, Joseph, David. Jesus is called the Good Shepherd; not only did he know his sheep and his sheep, him, but he smelled good.

Cain and Abel aren't just interesting characters in the plot. They offer parallels to Adam and Jesus. Interesting, isn't it? The first son worked the land. He had sin crouching at his heart and a warning from G to do what is right. Yet, he ignored the sage advice.

The second son was an innocent shepherd whose offering was acceptable to G, killed by his brother despite having been a righteous man. Agh! I'm giving away the plot.

In the course of time Cain brought some of the fruits of the soil as an offering to the LORD. But Abel brought fat portions from some of the firstborn of his flock. G looked with favor on Abel and his offering, but on Cain and his offering G did not look with favor. So Cain was very angry, and his face was downcast.

People often debate why G wasn't so crazy about Cain's offering. It's actually quite easy. G doesn't look at only actions because it is never about going through the motions. G looks at the heart using a flaming sword as a flashlight. Clearly something was bothering Cain if he could so easily become angry and downcast. I mentioned earlier how happiness is the sign of spiritual strength. Well, Cain needed to go to the gym more. Bitterness imprisons its keeper. Ironically, the only person who can open the door to freedom is the one who is incarcerated. As long as Cain held tight to the bitterness in his heart, he was susceptible to sin and simply could not escape its hold. If you could converse on a regular basis with the Creator of everything, what could be so bad and would make you so angry? Maybe Abel was the kid that mom liked best, but who cares? If you are doing your best and you are doing right, then you should be happy for—not jealous of—another person. It is kind of the prodigal son story again.

> Then G said to Cain, "Why are you angry? Why is your face downcast? If you do what is right, will you not be accepted? But if you do not do what is right, sin is crouching at your door; it desires to have you, but you must master it."

G does two main things here. First, G points out that "if" Cain did what is right, he would be accepted. The fact that he wasn't accepted flat-out tells you a lot about Cain. Second, G warns Cain here. You can almost picture G as a kung fu master, encouraging the student to discipline mind and body. I think the word *grasshopper* originally concluded G's sentence. I can't remember. Critical to any situation when a human feels bad is refraining from acting on that feeling. G warns that even if you *feel* angry or downcast, you must *do* what is right. You can *feel* what you want, but you *control* how you act. This is how you master sin.

G tells Cain that sin is waiting to pounce on him. This part intrigues me. There are so many humans who argue, "If G exists, why is there pain and suffering in the world?" Yet these same people never posit that parents must not exist because children get hurt. Parents constantly inundate their children with comments like "Don't touch that, it's hot." "Don't run with scissors." "Don't flush the cat."

Yet, sometimes children get burned, poked, or severely scratched by an angry pet. That the child got hurt does not mean the parent doesn't exist. It simply means the child made a choice with a consequence. Granted, sometimes people suffer at the hands of other people's bad choices. Sometimes people do bad or reckless things. Consequences ensue. That people have the choice to do something bad doesn't diminish the existence of G. That people get hurt because other people do bad things does not diminish the existence of G. G never promised you would be pain free, much like a parent would never promise a child that the child would have a pain-free life. But both figures will be there if their children get hurt, to hold them and love them and help them through the pain.

I remember once watching a mother sitting in bed crying at the recent loss of her elderly father. He succumbed to a long battle with cancer. She had loved her father very much. She sat in bed longing for one more chance to express her deep and sincere love and gratitude for all he had given her throughout her life. Her father's spirit sat imperceptibly beside her, touching her heart, trying to console her. He whispered, "Shh. Everything is okay, I am here." Then from the next room, the mother's small son cried out in a nightmare. The mother immediately jumped from her bed and ran to her sobbing child. She went to the bedside and gently lifted the boy into her arms. She softly rocked the boy back and forth and whispered, "Shh. Everything is okay, I am here."

For that moment the mother's sadness departed. She didn't even think of her own pain. She was able to find comfort in giving comfort. The child's sobbing slowed. As the child rested in the arms of the mother who loved him so dearly, he calmed. She calmed. This is what G is to us. G never promises a life of no pain. When there is pain, G holds you gently, strokes your heart, and whispers, "Shh. Everything is okay, I am here."

Have you ever seen a dad and child holding hands as they cross a street or a busy parking lot? While the child reaches out for the father's hand, it is not the child's grip on the dad that will save her from danger; it is the father's grip on the child that offers protection. It is the father who will help the child when she stays close.

G is always there, in the good and the bad. During hard times, many people ask, "Where is G?" G never hides. If you ever wonder where G is during the midst of suffering, look. Look closely. Look at the footage of the Twin Towers falling. Look at the police officers, the firefighters, the rescue workers, the volunteers selflessly giving of their time, energy, and strength. Walk into a hospital and wail over the illness and death throughout. Then look closely. Notice the doctors, nurses, aides, and staff who shuffle among patients to provide comfort and relief. Look at any situation where it appears evil is thriving, then look closely. If you cannot find the good, perhaps that is why you were put in that situation; to bring the good forth. If you can't *see* the good, *be* the good.

> Now Cain said to his brother Abel, "Let's go out to the field." And while they were in the field, Cain attacked his brother Abel and killed him."

Cain is now un-Abel.

Then G said to Cain, "Where is your brother Abel?"

Again, G loves to ask those questions the answers of which are already known. I suppose you humans do that too. Especially those of you who are parents.

"Where do you think you are going?"
"Who do you think you are talking to?"
"Do you expect me to believe that?"

"I don't know," he replied. "Am I my brother's keeper?"

This line has received quite the notoriety. Many scholars take Cain's statement to mean pretty much "It's not my job to watch over him. You are the big G. It's your job." That is quite close to Cain's intent. Cain argues that if G is all-powerful and all-knowing—G should have done something about it. Flashback … flash forward, over to Adam for a second. When Adam got busted for eating the fruit, G confronted him. Adam said, "It was that woman *you* put here with me." Adam not only threw Eve under the bus, he threw G under the bus as well. "*You* put her here with me." Flash forward to Cain and Able. After Cain killed Able, G confronted him. Cain stated, "Isn't looking after people *your* job?" Cain took on the sins of his father. You never heard Adam state, "Oops, my bad. I really should own-up to my mistake." And what was the result? Since Adam never admitted his sin, in essence, Adam marked the poison as "candy." Cain thought it was a safe defense—blame G. The sin of the parent now flowed to the child—except now the sin was exacerbated. Instead of exercising self-control, some humans simply look to—or plead with—G to stop the consequences.

Ah, consequences. You humans have attempted to seize dominion over those for some time. You have dominion over the earth but not over consequences. The knowledge of good and evil you have received has allowed you creative means to divert consequences for your personal benefit but not control the larger, lasting effects. You use your knowledge to avoid or delay consequences as opposed to correcting behavior. There was a time in history when people assigned god-qualities to the mysterious. The movement of the celestial bodies, the wind, the rain, water levels in the river, the growth and birth of human life were all mysteries. Many humans worshiped the independent items by assigning gods to them. There were gods of sun, moon, water, earth, fertility, stone, green clovers, pink hearts, orange stars, blue diamonds…. While one large group, dare I say a majority, arbitrarily worshiped independent facets of nature, there was a minority that opposed this view. They worshiped the One, the One who created the sun, moon, life, the universe, and everything. The minority were often oppressed for their controversial view that there is but one G, who created all and knows all.

As time went on and humans cultivated the Tree of Knowledge, they learned the science behind much of nature and how nature could benefit each individual person. Knowledge properly removed the god classifications from each natural element, but it also stripped away the value of the creation itself. Man will say, "I no longer need to pray to the sun, for I know its schedule. I no longer need to pray for rain, because I can calculate its expected arrival. I no longer need to pray to the god of fertility, because I can see a doctor." The shift will be from making many gods for each human to worship to making each human a god. Yet there will still be that same constant minority as in days of old. There will still be that group in the background who will be oppressed for the controversial view that there is but one G, who created all and knows all.

Over thousands of years, gods will come and go; atheism, agnosticism, and uncertainty will morph; but there will always be a constant group of people—crossing borders, nationalities, races, creeds, gender, and time—who will hold tight to the truth of the existence of one G.

Cain knew G. What Cain didn't appreciate was how much power to master sin was vested within him. He could have been a hero. These days, any story can be told and any facts woven into heroic brocades. But the biggest heroes are the people who stop doing bad and the people who do good in the face of adversity—a hero isn't always the man in the middle of combat. It is easy to shoot when you are fired upon. In the middle of a heated combat scene, the hero isn't the one who simply shoots when fired upon; the hero is the one who puts the greater good before personal benefit. But the heroes often overlooked are the parents who can lovingly speak to their rebellious teenagers when the teens rant or yell, the employees who work hard at jobs they loathe because they need to support their families; the mothers who get no sleep because they cleaned up the vomit four times last night; the teenagers who do what they know is right despite ridicule from their friends. These are the heroes of the world. These people, who endure everyday trials with amazing patience and grace, are the people to be championed, but their stories do not make headlines or talk shows. It is the one-off fireworks display that captivates humans, but the fireworks display is an ethereal show with nothing remaining but ash.

The little things, the ordinary things, create the miracles. The single grains of sand that contribute to the beach, the single blades of grass that comprise the fields, the single trees that contribute to the forests. If you don't believe me, eat a piece of chocolate every hour. They can be little, but at some point, the consequences will kick in, as evidenced by your bathroom scale. One snide comment can shift a perception entirely. One simple kindness can brighten a day. Consider one breath. You have lots of those each day. When they stop, someone will miss them more than they will miss your fireworks display.

Have you ever been bitten by a lion? A blue whale? An alligator? A mosquito? Maybe you can answer yes to the first three questions; I suppose there are a few people who could—maybe. Jonah? But they don't sell whale repellent. It is the little things that can build up or break down. You will connect with family and friends not by one-off, spectacular events, not the new toy, phone, car, or show, but by the consistency of your actions. If those actions do not have reassurance, praise, and love, it is not G who failed—although G gets blamed for quite a lot.

Humans are so good at blaming and judging G. A lot of people even think they could fill the position better. People wonder why there are those who do not want children but keep producing offspring while others want children but are infertile. Add to this conundrum of the hordes of orphans scattered throughout the world who are longing for parents. Why are there people with large homes and big yards; yet in some areas dozens of people are crammed into a hovel? Why do some people waste plates of food away at the all-you-can-eat buffet while others are starving? It is as if these people believe G loves them but just has a funny way of showing it.

The mere presentation of the question provides the answer. G set a giant smorgasbord of life events and things for the whole world. You have to share.

Think about a large dinner, maybe Thanksgiving, Christmas, or some other major feast with lots of people. If you sit down at the table and there is a bowl of potatoes in front of you, you do not mourn the loss of the stuffing because it may be located at the other end of the table. You know that the entire bowl or plate of anything is not meant for just you. Yes, it looks good. Yes, it is tasty. You still don't require the entire bowl. You are expected to take what you need to sample, maybe indulge a little, and then share. You don't seize the potatoes, dump the entire contents on your plate, and then proceed to do the same with every other side dish within your reach. Even if you think Uncle Todd is going to hoard all the cranberry sauce, you don't panic by grabbing the nearest side dish and refusing to pass it.

On the same note, just because you have the potatoes and can pass them to the next potato recipient doesn't make you better than anyone else at the table. You are not a greater person for sharing, nor are you a lesser person for needing to have the food shared. Everyone comes to the table as equals. Those who hold the dishes are not better than others who are waiting to receive. If you sat down and dumped the entire spread onto your plate (assuming you had a very large plate) while those around you were hungry, you would never purport to say, "Isn't G here? Let G feed you. Am I the hostess or the mother that I need to feed these guests?" Whether you are the hostess or the mother is irrelevant. The answer is "Yes."

It's easy to see this need to give and take when your world is limited to the table, but now you need to expand your view of just how big this table really is. Yes, there are people who hold the bowl of potatoes, even though they dislike them; there also are those at the other end waiting for the potatoes to come. There is everything humans need to be satiated. But if you cling to one dish, you cannot open your hands to give or to receive more and different food, nor can anyone else receive until you let go. Until you let go of the potatoes, you will never experience the main dish. You are your brother's keeper. You are the hostess. G invited *everyone* to the table. No exceptions. Don't be a potato-hoarder.

> G said, "What have you done? Listen! Your brother's blood cries out to me from the ground. Now you are under a curse and driven from the ground, which opened its mouth to receive your brother's blood from your hand. When you work the ground, it will no longer yield its crops for you. You will be a restless wanderer on the earth." Cain said to the Lord, "My punishment is more than I can

bear. Today you are driving me from the land, and I will be hidden from your presence; I will be a restless wanderer on the earth, and whoever finds me will kill me."

The original text actually has the word *blood* as plural,[72] suggesting that Abel's offspring that never had the chance to be born cried out with their father-to-have-been. The harm committed against one person hurts not only that person but many others. Humanity is so intertwined that by killing one man, you are killing a race.

This passage is also proof that G made many, not just Adam and Eve. Granted, people often feel that their parents are going to kill them for something they did, but Cain isn't worried about Mom and Dad here. He's worried about the masses he may meet as he wanders. There were others.

But speaking of Mom and Dad…. Parents rule over their children for only a time. There is that tiny window of about a decade and a half whereby parents have authority over their children. Parents often confuse authority with control. Parents were never meant to control children, and just about any parent will tell you that you can't—just as G doesn't control people. G trains you, G corrects you, but ultimately, it is the humans who have the choice about how to live their lives. Parents need to do the same.

There is a psalm that states that "children … are like arrows in a warrior's hands. How joyful is the man whose quiver is full of them!" This sounds like such a dreamy proverb. Any *expectant* parent would be quick to agree. However, the parent of a challenging child or a teenager may be more inclined to change the proverb to "Children … are like arrows in a warrior's hands. How joyful is the man whose bow is loaded!"

The Bible provides tips on dealing with adolescents. There are hundreds of great books out there on dealing with youth, but I have found that the most successful approaches were present in the Bible well before copyright law came into play.

First, let's set the stage. Many parents get frustrated with their kids and are convinced that G is somehow forcing them to serve

---

[72] The word would have been bloods and have nothing to do with gangs.

penance. They take solace that they will be able to skip right over purgatory and go straight to heaven after having raised some rather spirited kids. G totally gets what you are going through. I stand firmly beside the premise that Lucifer was fifteen when he rebelled against G. I know many parents feel that their child is actually meeting with Lucifer on the side to get tips on how to be more conniving—only the parents aren't sure who is teaching whom. Rest assured, this is totally normal. The most important thing a parent can do is follow some fundamental scriptures and not commit any felonies.

Adam and Eve missed the most critical element in parenting, teaching your kids about G. Scripture states that if you spare the rod, you spoil the child. Some parents thought a rod was a weapon with which they were supposed to beat children. While you may sometimes feel like doing that, G never meant that. In fact, Psalm 23 says, "Your rod and your staff, they comfort me." Well, a rod wouldn't be very comforting if you knew you were going to be beaten with it. I'm just saying…. A lot of things comfort me, but not a club intended to strike me, regardless of the motivation. If G's rod was coming at you with the intention of a beating—I am pretty confident you would not feel comforted.

Isaiah describes the rod quite well. The rod isn't used to *strike*, but to *weigh* on humans. It refers to that part of the yoke that rests on the burdened animal. When raising children, parents should not spare the rod—the yoke—of G. Jesus will provide more insight on the true yoke of G by stating that his burden is easy and his yoke is light. But if children are not given the yoke of G, if they don't have boundaries, how can they walk a straight and narrow path?

The boundaries, the rules, can't be a collection of a personal, parental manifesto. Even though parents *believe* they are correct, and may believe they totally understand what their kids are facing—they don't. Even with similar histories, no parent has had the exact life of their child, so they don't truly understand them, although admitting this can be hard. Equally, kids have not been through what adults have; they don't understand their parents, either. Part of that misunderstanding is the kid trying to figure out if and why something is right or wrong. Parents can't issue edicts based solely on what *they* believe is right or wrong; after all, even parents can be wrong.

The standard for morality cannot be simply the parent's preference; because when the child becomes an adult, the standard will be whatever the now-grown child personally determines it to be. If parents teach their children morality devoid of a moral law-giver, then morality falls when the parents' credibility falls. And parents' credibility *will* fall. By nature, humans are fallible.

A great example of this is Hitler. Can you imagine what Hitler's mom would have said to change his behavior? She could have yelled until the cows came home that he needed to listen to her because she was his mom. He may have countered that, because he was führer, she needed to listen to him. He now wielded a title, a perceived power, an alleged authority. There came a point in time when mom could do nothing to stop the bad behavior by appealing to her own authority. To what could she have appealed? Easy—an authority above them both.

I am not saying children are like Hitler—although there may be parents who disagree—but you can point to a higher authority to support your claim that his behavior was immoral. You must be able to do this with your children as well. The earlier you start instructing your children about the yoke of G, the more they have time to digest, ingest, and even throw up the concepts. This is fine. Even Timothy[73] said to "test everything and hold on to the good." Kids need to test; kids will test. A parent's job is not to stop children from testing and questioning—it is to teach them to recognize and hold on to the good. It is never too late to start.

Suppose I pull out a board game and ask you, "Do you want to play by the rules of the creator of the game or by the rules that I created?"[74] Odds are, you are going to want to play by the rules made by the creator of the game. The rules of the one who created the game are fair and intended to make an interesting game not benefiting any one person. My personal rules may or may not be fair; chances are, they will benefit me.

---

[73] Real credit goes to Paul but now you know what book to read.

[74] For instance, no other angel will play Monopoly by my rules because my rules mandate that I get the equivalent of $2 million for passing Go—and Railroads and Chance and Community Chest and Utilities.

By electing to fall on the yoke of G, you are telling children, "Fine, you don't play by my rules; I won't play by your rules. Let's both play by these objective rules."

If parents aren't playing by objective rules, kids will begin to see the parents as inconsistent. If you want to know what it is like for teenagers dealing with parents, play a game of tag with a seven year old. Just as you get ready to tag the kid, he screams, "Wait, time out!" or "This is base!" (pointing at any particular object he happens to be physically touching at that moment) or "No tag backs!" The rules get introduced as the game is played. It can get frustrating. Just when you think you've got it down, a new twist appears that seems to benefit only the person making the rule. This is how teenagers see parents. However, if you set the rules out in advance—rules that the Creator of the game drafted—then the game becomes easier to play. There will be times when a rule benefits one party, but there are times when the other benefits, as well. The game is easier to play and is actually more fun to play.

Keep in mind, though, the Word of G can be a double-edged sword. Parents who wield the directive for children to obey G's rules must be willing to subject themselves to the same authority. G provides advice on how to raise children, but if parents disregard their own scriptural obligations, they teach their children that it is okay to be hypocritical. You can't expect kids to play by the rules their parents aren't playing by.

The earlier parents begin teaching Scripture and the soundness of Scripture, the easier it becomes to avoid the power struggle. This doesn't mean parents with spirited older youth should throw their hands up; it just means they need to unclench their fists and acknowledge their own shortcomings. In fact, when your kids see the changes that G makes in you—their parents—the more they are going to be willing to play by G's rules. When kids see their parents becoming more humble, less stressed, gentler, less explosive—the more they want to be a part of that change. Bringing your children to G is precisely the end goal of every parent[75].

---

[75] Matthew 19:14. Jesus calls the children, not only the bright-eyed toddlers, but eye-rolling teenagers, as well.

No one is perfect, even Scripture declares that "all have sinned".[76] If parents pretend to be perfect because of the mere fact they are parents, they are not being true to themselves or their children. If parents fail to acknowledge when they have fallen short, they blur morality for their children and teach the most dangerous of all habits—the justification of sin. It is mixing dinner in with dessert, because it's all going to the same place. It is the combining of the holy and the secular. It's the labeling of poison as candy. Children are more likely to carry that sin forward in their lives because if it was okay for their parents, it is okay for them. They may even justify a little bit more. It becomes the slippery slope through the generations that spirals only downward—just as Cain exhibited Adam's trait of shifting blame. If a parent opens the door for a bad excuse, a kid will kick it open for a worse one. Pick your battles, admit weaknesses. Be imperfect. It is okay. You know what people who sin are? Human.

That is the beauty of grace. Parents are not expected to be perfect. When a parent is out of line, the first thing that parent should do is admit the shortcoming and work to repair it. Telling a child that you are going to work at giving up smoking, drinking, cursing, philandering, overworking, underworking, or—insert a particular vice here—is sharing the rod by agreeing to play by the rules you demand of the kids. It is a journey to G that you can take together.

It is also critical when dealing with anyone, especially children, that your yes be yes and your no be no. Anything more than that is trouble, inconsistent, and gives the child a great deal of power—power without restraint. It's as if parents live in a missile silo and tell the children to push a button, any button.

Tell your children what is expected and tell them the consequences of disobedience. Don't increase the consequences when you are particularly angry or having a bad day. Don't lessen the consequences because the child has now decided to behave well. Let your yes be yes and your no be no; anything else is just annoying.

Many times I have seen parents threaten their children with months of grounding, only to slack up after a few days. Kids should never be grounded for months; it is cruel and unusual

---

[76] Check out three Romans—er, Romans 3.

punishment—for the parent. Before a parent issues verdicts and decrees, there must be thought and planned enforcement behind the words.

When your child is in trouble, try to imagine getting pulled over for speeding. Can you imagine what it would be like if the police officer started screaming at you? What if he said, "That's it! Not only am I going to write you a ticket, I'm going to tell your friends about what you have done. I'm going to double the fine and take away your license." Yet the next time you are caught speeding, he says, "Well, we all make mistakes." You aren't going to focus on whether or not you speed as much as wondering what will happen if the nut job pulls you over. You may not appreciate speeding as even being an offense because of the inconsistency with which it is handled. In fact, getting caught may not even serve as a deterrent because there are odds that you can get away with speeding regardless. The odds are you will be able to talk yourself out of the consequence. Why? Because every teenager is a little lawyer and will herald "You let me get away with it before, so why not now?" This puts the parent in the position of stating they either messed up before or are messing up now. You are changing the rules mid game! The parent now takes the witness stand.

I am pretty confident that any teenager could pass the bar exam. They generally have opening arguments, cross examination, and the closing argument mastered before you even ask them why they are late. When they hit adolescence, children may begin to engage adults in more complex battles. Launch an accusation at a teenager, and within minutes you may be answering interrogatories. Once the teen assumes the position of prosecutor, authority dissolves and power struggle ensues. This is always an interesting event. I'm not sure what is more interesting—the fact that the adolescents initiate a battle or that the parents indulge the request. It is easy when the child is young to see how foolish an argument would be. You couldn't really see a parent and a child screaming "Am not!" "Am too!" "Am not!" "Am too!" But when the child develops a more articulate vocabulary, parents may allow this fight to happen.

Engaging in fights devalues parental authority. The results can be even more disastrous once this stark realization hits parents who are now fighting at the level of their child (regardless of age). The knee-jerk reaction of parents who suddenly realize they have reduced themselves to adolescence is to drop the nuclear bomb of control, which tends to result in strange punishments like never allowing children to leave the house again or taking every single possession out of the children's rooms. The only thing such drastic parenting actions accomplish is heralding the parents' lack of control and complete frustration. Interestingly enough, this provides some comfort to children who were in the wrong, because now everyone involved is in the wrong. It is difficult to punish someone for dirty hands when your hands are also unclean. Misery loves company. Your kids may have screwed up, but they got *you* to feel bad about it.

When your child—or anyone for that matter—messes up, pull him or her over, write the ticket, and end it.

Of course, it is necessary to correct children.[77] When a child of any age is engaging in sinful activities—who better than the parent to call out the matter? The Book of Proverbs states that parents should discipline, or properly instruct, their child, as the parents may save that child from death. But calling out any shortcoming should always be done out of love and never to shame. Kind of like how Paul states it the fourth chapter of Corinthians: he doesn't write to shame but to "warn you as my dear children." Humility, grace, and respect should always be employed when calling out shortcomings. "Long comings" can be loud and obnoxious, but not shortcomings.

You must correct your children. Your role is to parent, not to be a friend.[78] There are dozens of people auditioning to be your kids' friends. Someone simply must fill the role of parent. One day your kids will grow up and be self-responsible. At that point, there is a natural segue from parent to friend.

When it comes to children, parents must learn, teach, and apply the yoke of G calmly and consistently, fulfilling this responsibility

---

[77] Proverbs 29.

[78] Of course, if one of their friends wants to step up to the plate and be a real parent, then you can consider friendship.

and not tiring the child with words or punishment. All instruction, correction, and interaction should be done in love.[79]

Children want their parents' love. Both parents. If you skip forward and read the story of Jacob and Esau, you will notice that the book tells you Isaac loved Esau and Rebekah loved Jacob. This is a huge problem. If the parents start divvying up their favor among the kids, the children will not only rebel against the parents, as Jacob and Esau did, but there will also be some serious sibling rivalry, like the rivalry between Jacob and Esau. Children sometimes will test to see if you can still love them when they do bad acts. You must love your children equally, regardless of their actions.

Don't get me wrong—as a parent you may very well connect more with one child than another. But connecting is a lot like getting dressed; sure, you have that T-shirt that just feels awesome and looks okay—contrary to what your spouse may say—but you know there will be times when you want to wear something nicer. Maybe something fancier, maybe something simpler. Even though you may think one child relates better, all children bring something into your life—something you need.[80] They each need to be recognized for that contribution.

This leads to a similar issue. Parents must empower their children. Give them the tools, but don't build for them. Empowering is found in responsibility. Parents should not be doing things for children that children can do for themselves. Do you find yourself picking up after your children all the time? Why? Do you feel exhausted after making dinner, setting the table, clearing the table, doing the laundry—all after you have come home from work? If you, the parent, feel stressed or overwhelmed, and you have a child who has no idea how to do any of these things, you are doing both of you a strong disservice. Now, don't expect perfection, but expect help.

Your children should enter adulthood knowing how to fully take care of themselves, not only physically, but emotionally and spiritually as well. You will not always be there for your kids. You have to

---

[79] See Colossians 3 or 1 Corinthians 13 (Since it is "1" Corinthians, perhaps it should be 1 Corinthian?)

[80] And no, I am not necessarily speaking about tolerance or patience.

teach them to draw on the one source that will always be there—G. You get them to G by love.

Your love must be unconditional. There simply is no way around it. Don't love them only when they are good or when they do what you want. Love them as G has loved you and as G has requested. Don't limit your love to your children. Expand the love beyond your immediate family and friends. Cultivate love and allow those seeds to scatter.

> But G said to him, "Not so; if anyone kills Cain, he will suffer vengeance seven times over." Then G put a mark on Cain so that no one who found him would kill him. So Cain went out from G's presence and lived in the land of Nod, east of Eden."[81]

G stated that no one could harm Cain for his crime. G knew that when people began to exact justice on their own, they would quickly become mercenaries.[82] Add to that society's slowing separation from G, and people would become merciless, moral-less mercenaries, more or less. By not allowing the people to take revenge, G was mitigating the bloodshed.

Cain left the presence of G. It is never good to leave the presence of G. Ever.

Teaching and learning G's Word is the primary objective of any parent. It is a little feat to bring a person into the world; it is an amazing feat to bring a person into the world to come. Any physical act can accomplish the former. It takes spiritual weightlifting to accomplish the latter.

Had Adam and Eve impressed the value of relationship with G, Cain would not have feared the masses that might harm him and would have recognized his true loss—living outside of the presence of G. Cain lost the most important thing in life but missed it. Cain didn't fear G; he feared death.

---

[81] Nod, just south of Winken and Blinken.

[82] If people were allowed to exact judgment on their own, civilization wouldn't have made it a decade.

There will be a time in history when knights would decry the act of ambushing an enemy as immoral because it did not allow the enemy the chance to make the peace with G. Funny, these knights did not fear death; they feared G. If only Cain had been so wise.

Parents must teach their children to think beyond the finite time on earth and shift to the infinite. It can seem like an overwhelming task, especially if the parent isn't sure of his or her own faith. How can a parent demonstrate the value of G in their child's life?

Imagine your friend wants you to meet her grandmother. You agree. Your friend then provides you with sixty-six books in small type printed on thin paper and says, "Here. Read this. It will tell you all about her." This may cause you to reconsider significantly just how much you want to meet Grandma. In fact, you may simply be too busy or too uninterested to entertain such an undertaking for this grandma. How great can she be? Even if you do happen to flip through the book, you find metaphors that you don't get, events that seem unreal, and even some naughty poetry—which actually might be interesting if you could figure out those darn metaphors.

Your teenager is not interested in homework. That is what happens when humans try to teach people about G from a text perspective only. G becomes synonymous with school, with study, with work and boredom. G becomes lackluster and potentially fictional. Don't give people a two-dimensional G; give them the three-dimensional G.

Now, suppose your friend comes to you and shows you all the amazing things her grandma taught her. You are shocked at how your friend seems to accomplish so much good in the time she has. You see her give to the poor, write to the prisoners, and help the orphans. Every time you see her, you wonder how she does all that. Your friend tells you that her grandmother taught her. Your friend is happy regardless of what is happening in her life. Even when things are going horribly, she is content. She tells you that her grandmother always takes care of her. Your friend is kind, gentle, and humble. You feel like a better person when you are with her. But your friend tells you she is nothing compared to her teacher—her grandma. You may begin to ask questions about what, exactly, Grandma teaches her. You may start to want to know more about

Grandma. Your friend gives you a book that Grandma wrote. You read it. You kind of get it. But seeing your friend's behavior, happiness, and actions draws you to want to know more. You will be more encouraged to seek out Grandma when you see that knowing Grandma has real effects.

One critical point to note: even if you finally get to meet grandma, your relationship will be different than your friend's relationship. Ultimately, you want to meet her because she is amazing and can transform your life. But no one can control or dictate how that relationship will develop. It is the same with G.

Seeking G's presence is tantamount to every human life. Heaven is the place where the individual meets the divine, and it should be a quest not satiated until heaven is completely within you.

There is a story about four men who believed in a place called heaven where the heart is light and love is abundant. The four men set out to find this place called heaven.

The first man had to venture through a vast desert with scorching heat, blistering winds, and freezing nights. His life seemed empty and devoid of everything. The loneliness that surrounded him was great, but he never lost faith he would find heaven. It was this faith that allowed him to successfully endure many hardships. After persevering for a great deal of time, he came to a high wall and proceeded to scale the wall. When he reached the top, he was overjoyed, because he looked down and could see heaven. He jumped down and reveled in paradise.

The second man had to travel through a dense jungle full of strange creatures and plants and eerie noises. Everything seemed unfamiliar and even scary. The brush was so dense he could barely see five feet in front of him. The second man grew weary at his ordeal but knew that he would find heaven. Finally, he too came upon a large wall and scaled the wall. Upon reaching the top, he saw heaven. He jumped down and joined the first man in paradise.

The third man also wanted to find heaven. He traveled through a violent city. He faced gangs, drugs, and brutality, but he stayed strong in his quest. After a long and hard ordeal, he finally came to the great wall. He climbed the wall, like others before him. Upon reaching the top, he saw heaven. He joyfully jumped into paradise.

The fourth man set out on his quest. He suffered many afflictions, much like those you suffer. Like the others before him, his afflictions were a result of the environment he was in. Whether he sought to find heaven or not, the pain and suffering would still happen. He was able to move through the suffering because he had faith that the environment in which he currently found himself was not permanent. There was something bigger and better than the deserts, the jungles, the cities, and any other place a person may be situated. With this knowledge, he happily endured the challenges until such time as he came to a great wall. He scaled the wall. Upon reaching the top, he saw paradise. *But* unlike the previous three men, the fourth man did not jump into paradise. He scaled back down the wall and went back to the place from which he came so that he might lead others to heaven.

Parents simply must embark on the journey to find G so that they can go back and show their children the way. Knowing that the trappings of the world are nothing compared to the beauty that awaits you, provides the strength to sustain you even in the most difficult of times.

> Cain made love to his wife, and she became pregnant and gave birth to Enoch. Cain was then building a city, and he named it after his son Enoch. To Enoch was born Irad, and Irad was the father of Mehujael, and Mehujael was the father of Methushael, and Methushael was the father of Lamech. Lamech married two women, one named Adah and the other Zillah. Adah gave birth to Jabal; he was the father of those who live in tents and raise livestock. His brother's name was Jubal; he was the father of all who play stringed instruments and pipes. Zillah also had a son, Tubal-Cain, who forged all kinds of tools out of bronze and iron. Tubal-Cain's sister was Naamah."

Are you still awake? Whew. Close one. Remember G doesn't do superfluous. There is a reason for this seemingly uninteresting passage. Yes, G does provide facts for the mere sake of historical accuracy but also keep in mind that Scripture is an invitation to learn more about G and relationships in general. If you were to do research, the etymology of the names, like the river discussion earlier, you will find some interesting information.

Granted, names can carry more than one meaning, especially when you are dealing with the Hebrew language which can have flexible application. For instance, some possible translations for the names above are: Lamech: powerful, servant; Adah: ornament, dawn; Zillah: shadow, grow dark; Jabal: leading, shepherd; Jubal: joyful sound, jubilee; Tubal-Cain: blacksmith, interaction with world economy; and Naamah: pleasure.

Now knowing some possible meanings of the names, the paragraph you just read can be re-read as follows: "The powerful servant married two wives, one Light and the other Darkness. Light gave birth to a Leader; he was the father of nomads and herdsman. His brother was Jubilee and the father of musicians. Darkness brought forth the blacksmith who forged all kinds of tools out of bronze and iron. Darkness' sister was Pleasure.

Again, I'm not here to tell you exactly what everything means. I just want you to get a better understanding about what you may be missing when you read Genesis.

> Lamech said to his wives, "Adah and Zillah, listen to me; wives of Lamech, hear my words. I have killed a man for wounding me, a young man for injuring me. If Cain is avenged seven times, then Lamech seventy-seven times."

This passage supports the contention that, absent repentance and personal accountability, sin flows through the generations. Cain's great-great-great-great-grandson, Lamech, killed a man and a boy for injuring him; that's pretty harsh retribution. He expresses no remorse, he doesn't make any notable attempts to atone for his wrong, and he doesn't call on G. He tells his wives.

Lamech, recognizing that his sin was worthy of punishment, provided his own permission for forgiveness—devoid of G. While G told Cain that men would not seek retribution against him for his crime; Lamech bestowed the same protection to himself. If, for killing one man, Cain had sevenfold protection, then for killing a man and a boy, Lamech would have exponentially more. He has sinned the greater and therefore requires greater forgiveness. But while great sin does require great forgiveness, forgiveness is more than a self-proclamation to noninvolved third parties.

Jesus specifically references the seven and the seventy-seven of Lamech in the book of Matthew.[83] A man asked how many times to forgive a person who sins. Jesus said, "Not seven times, but seventy-seven times." Jesus' statement supports the mitigating tactics employed by G when Cain committed his horrible offense. Humans were not bestowed the right to exact vengeance upon sinners. Vengeance belongs only to G and is not a right afforded mortals, lest the masses destroy themselves. This actually plays out in the lineage of Cain. His offspring's violence continues to increase, and all of Cain's offspring are annihilated during the great flood.[84]

> Adam made love to his wife again, and she gave birth to a son and named him Seth, saying, "G has granted me another child in place of Abel, since Cain killed him." Seth also had a son, and he named him Enosh. At that time people began to call on the name of the LORD.

It is this last sentence which is of greatest import. Notice that when Adam sinned, G confronted him. When Eve sinned, G confronted her. When Cain sinned, there was G confronting again. When Lamech sinned—G is noticeably absent. G did not confront the sinner. The time had now come when the people had to call on G.

A change occurred but the change is not in G. Some people think that G changed drastically from the Old to the New Testament. They believe G was harsh, judgmental, and cruel in the Old Testament but loving and kind in the New. This is akin saying "When I was seven, my parents were so mean. When I broke the rules they would

---

[83] I even referenced Jesus referencing it when I referenced G's ideas on relating with people.

[84] Noah comes from the lineage of Seth, Cain's brother ... who will be appearing momentarily.

yell, pop my bottom or put me in time out. Now, that I'm thirty they never do that anymore. They sure have changed." The parents didn't change; the *relationship* changed. When you are younger, your parents try to impress upon you the importance of goodness before you move away. It is this way with G.

On a similar note, some will argue that the Old Testament portrays G as cruel and heartless. Actually, humans just reaped what they had sown. Think about it, when the angel of death took the first born in Egypt, it was just a few decades after the pharaoh had ordered the execution of the Hebrew children. The Egyptians chose to exert their power over the Hebrews through death; the tables turned. At one point in history, the accuser *and the accuser's family* would suffer the intended fate of the accused if the accused was found innocent. When Daniel was released from the lion's den, King Darius ordered the accusers *and their families* thrown into the pit. Why? Because that was the standard. When G orders the same sentence, people are shocked and attribute moral failings to G. When humans reap what they sow, it isn't a cruel act of G. It is G pointing out that you should be cautious in your judgments as you may be subject to them.

Act 5: Genesis 5, Adam to Noah

This is the written account of Adam's family line. When G created mankind, G made them in the likeness of G. G created them male and female and blessed them. And G named them "Mankind" when they were created."

Ah, we have come full circle. I could go on forever; seriously, I really could go on forever because I have no time constraints, but it appears I have passed the creation and begun moving into—well, destruction. For the record, it isn't as though G made a mistake and decided to wipe the board clean with a flood. Mankind had already set the wheels for self-destruction in motion. Just like with Adam and Eve, there are consequences for sin. The great flood shouldn't be an exercise in analyzing how G wiped out those who were already wiping out each other—but how G separated and protected the faithful.

This particular passage, while segueing into the story of Noah, again repeats what was stated early in the creation process. G didn't make "a" male and female. G made "them." "Mankind."

While there is nothing I would enjoy more than regaling you with insights on the story of Noah, I will save that story for another time. I must, however, regale you with clarity on the Tree of Life. I can't leave the garden and leave out this critical tree.

Act 6: The Tree of Life

The Tree of Life has been debated for centuries. It is actually quite simple. Scripture will repeatedly refer to the Tree of Life equating to wisdom in general; but how about wisdom, specifically? This five-branched tree stands before mankind to date. The branches have individual names: Genesis, Exodus, Deuteronomy, Leviticus, and Numbers.[85] If you really swing from these limbs of this tree, you will find the blueprint of wisdom as revealed and fulfilled in the Messiah—the ultimate path to eternal life. See, on its face, Genesis presents knowledge of Adam and Eve. On a deeper level, Genesis provides insight in obtaining wisdom and identifying the Messiah.[86]

G had to tell you about the Messiah. G had to give foreshadowing. Absent the foreshadowing, the timing, and the insight—how would

---

[85] Also known as Torah or the beginning of Old Testament. In Hebrew, the book titles actually translate as "In the Beginning" (Genesis), "Names" (Exodus), "He Called" (Leviticus), "In the Wilderness" (Numbers), and "Words" (Deuteronomy).

[86] Actually, most of the Old Testament points to the Messiah.

you recognize the Messiah[87] when he comes? How do you know the Messiah?

Believers should be careful to understand what they believe. Do not blindly follow other people—that's an Eve thing. Seek G. The path is provided in Scripture, and it will bring you closer to the Divine.

I do want to digress for a moment and state that it isn't just Christians who can blindly follow a belief. Atheists are equally guilty. The fundamental premise of atheism is that G doesn't exist. But ask an atheist "What is G?" Many will stammer and will be unable to define precisely what doesn't exist. If I told you that Wonkuoy doesn't exist and you asked me "What is Wonkuoy?" It would be quite silly of me to not have a response. Sometimes atheists will redirect to the believer and ask for the believer's definition of G. It's a bit of a cop-out but workable.

I recommend that the believer state that "G is love." Start with the basics and with what you know. Define G with a core characteristic. If G equals love then most all atheists will concede love exists—even though they can't prove it.

Now expand the definition— "G is love, compassion, and inner-peace." Again, the atheist cannot prove the existence of any of these things but they would be hard-pressed in saying they don't exist. Perhaps they can wax philosophical about everything being an illusion, but in the end, most atheists marry people for other than purely scientific reasons and mourn the loss of a loved one. There are un-provable catalysts in their lives upon which they feel and act. Atheists love and feel compassion. They can't prove it, but they can't deny it.

---

[87] I can't say the name Messiah without saying the name Jesus. It's a real fun name to say here. At the invocation of the Name, all knees bend. Have you ever gone up behind someone and gently tapped him or her on the back of the knee? Sometimes the knee gives a little, and the person stoops in response. That's what happens when Jesus' name is said. It's not a bad reaction, or even an annoying one. It's the same type of reaction you get when you try to look at a beautiful sunrise, especially over the water. It is so awesome and colorful and amazing. You can see the general form, but there is usually a lot of squinting involved. You aren't bothered by the squinting. The glory of what you want to see simply triggers a peripheral response, overridden by a greater respect for the experience.

An atheist could argue that if G is simply love, compassion, and inner peace,[88] then just call G that. However, that argument equates to calling that yummy dessert "egg-sugar-flour-mixture" versus the truly more appropriate descriptor of "cake."[89] The sum is greater than the parts.

I know I mentioned proof of G earlier but, weirdly enough, the whole "proving" argument tends to be the fallback position for atheists. They will say G doesn't exist and then state that they do not need to offer any proof for the assertion because you can't prove a negative and the burden of proof rests with the believer. This is a patent fallacy in logic. Atheists argue absent proof, the assertion cannot be true. If this is true, then the atheist's lack of proof for his or her assertion would equally discount that assertion. No human would like to have his or her doctor say "You don't have cancer. I don't need to run any tests because you don't have to prove a negative." You are going to want some serious investigatory work to be performed to support the conclusion.

Suppose a woman told a man "You don't have any money but I don't have to prove it." For her statement to be true, she will have to have seen every bank account, safety deposit box and balance sheet of the man's. She would also have to know what was under his bed, in his wallet, or in his pockets. For her to make such a bold statement, she would have had to engage in an exhaustive search to support her position or be nothing short of omnipotent. Maybe he has a piggy bank at his cabin in the woods, or maybe he has some loose change in his sofa. He knows he has money, even if he can't produce it during the discussion. The notable distinction is that for a man to say that something exists because he has experienced it is quite different than for the woman to say it doesn't exist because she has not. For a person to say that something doesn't exist for anyone else because he or she hasn't personally experienced it is nothing short of pride. Just because *you* weren't in the forest when the tree fell doesn't mean others weren't surprised by the noise. In fact, the only way a

---

[88] I previously mentioned these thirteen attributes of G. See Exodus 34:6–7.

[89] It would also significantly drag down a conversation to simply repeat every attribute versus the final product.

person can legitimately claim there is no all-knowing, omnipotent being would be if they were, in fact, all-knowing and omnipotent.

Although, the mere fact that atheists unite to denounce something actually lends credibility to its existence. Think about how many other people gather on the premise that they collectively want to pronounce something doesn't exist? Why don't people unite as a-plaid-otter-ists or a-bicycling-sharks-ists? Quick! Name something that doesn't exist in nature![90] Hard, isn't it? Would you consider starting a club to advance your newly found cause of the non-existent? If something *does not* exist, you don't rally the troops to defeat it.[91] Unless your goal is simply to go offensive on those with a contrary belief.

What if someone told you they, in fact, saw a plaid otter? Do you argue harder against its existence or do you admit the possibility that someone has experienced something that you have not? This latter point would require a great deal of humility.

Atheists may define their belief—er—disbelief is disbelief in a "Creator." That would bring you back to the creation discussion earlier. Scientists concede that *something* came from *nothing*; many scientists go a step farther and admit to intelligent design. Scientists simply cannot explain the trigger of creation, the catalyst or *in what* the universe was created. The greatest minds in the world cannot explain the *how*, *why*, *in what* did creation occur; it is not surprising that they would disavow the *Who*.[92]

Remember, the universe is expanding. Let's go backwards in time so that the universe contracts to that point of singularity. *In what* did the Big Bang occur? Space is expanding. *Into what* is it expanding? If space gets bigger, it can't expand into more space else you haven't hit the boundary of space. Boggle your mind and try to imagine what was before the Big Bang. There was no space. Absent space and a rate of expansion or movement there could be no time. Time was created

---

[90] I already gave you plaid otters and bicycling sharks so you have to come up with something else.

[91] That would make for a funny battle cry "Quick men! We are being surrounded by something that isn't there!"

[92] Not the classic rock group.

when G made the universe. How old is the emptiness that existed before the Big Bang? Why did the Big Bang occur? Only religion can answer the *Why* and the *Who*. The premise of G as a Creator is not devoid of reason or of thought; in fact, it is the only logical solution.

Atheists may argue that there is no "higher power," but this means that each person is the highest power to themselves, and each person can subjectively define morality.

Morality is not and cannot be based on subjectivity. If it is, then the need for prisons, police, judges, and lawyers disappears.[93] After all, if one human believes it is okay to kill or steal and you disagree, then you are simply overpowering that person's belief with your personal opinion. You could never be upset by any other person's actions because every person is entitled to feel as he or she believes and to act on those beliefs. Really to hit this point home, if you truly believe each individual has the ability to define right and wrong for himself or herself, then you can never call Hitler an evil man. After all, he believed he was right; what makes you his boss? The rationale that each person gets to choose morality doesn't make anything right; it makes things muddy. It doesn't matter what Hitler believed. He was wrong. There is a higher law. Where there is a higher law, there is a *higher law Giver*.

The next argument is that right and wrong are determined by the collective. Morality morphs into popular opinion. Each grain of sand has its voice, and the sands would continue to shift in accordance with the ever-changing tide of popular opinion. Morality by democracy will fail. The number of Nazis exceeded the number of slain Jewish people. Sometimes the minority is right and the majority is wrong.

Most all humans would agree that the Holocaust was an atrocity, but how can someone make that claim without pointing to an objective standard of morality? You can't accuse someone else of being wrong simply because you say so. You would be just as guilty as the person you accuse. You must point to something bigger and greater than the both of you. If each person is independently right; then the

---

[93] The fact that many would actually like to see the lawyers vanish is not the point.

atheist, by his or her own argument, cannot tell any individual that he or she is wrong.

Some atheists reject that there is any point to anything. If that's the case, why bothering talking about it? Why bother even having the opinion? It's pointless.

What most atheists truly reject are the Christians who beat them with dead flashlights. Some people turn from the very thought of G because of the bad actions of people who purport to be believers. This is why G made it very clear that *all* people were sinners; so that people would not assign to G the hatred expressed by men.

But how does a *believer* define G? Even as an angel, I know the impossibility of such a task. But finite human minds want and need digestible explanations—not as the complete and final answer, but simply as an invitation to explore.

Scientifically speaking, G is what was before creation. G is the creator of the universe and omnipotent knower of what falls beyond. G is the Why, the How, the When, the What and the Who. G is the infinite, much like numbers. No human in his or her right mind would actually try to count every single number there is *before* trying to do math. G is the same way. Learn the basics. Learn the equations. The potential is limitless. You will never know everything there is to know about G, but you can learn enough to be empowered.

Philosophically speaking, G is the caster of shadows on the cave fall.[94] Humans may claim, "I think, therefore I am;"[95] G's claim is "I am." G is the *objective* morality to which every human must strive to be super; morality, not devoid of the weak, but in unity with weak.[96] G is the creator of the chicken *and* the egg. G is the sound of the tree falling in the forest, audible only to those who draw near and listen.

---

[94] See the Allegory of the Caves by Plato for more insight here.

[95] This was first coined by Descartes ... as in the thing that gets pulled by De-horse. To be clear, Descartes made a leap in his assertion. He believed that because there is thought, people exist. Technically, because there is thought, *thinking* exists.

[96] This is in contrast to the belief that the people can rise above and be better than other people and live devoid of a common morality. Did I mention that Nietzsche was dead?

Characteristically speaking, G is love and those twelve other traits found in Exodus. G has spoken through prophets and explicitly ordained the coming of the Messiah.

Practically speaking, G is the infinite being whose Word was made manifest in the person of Jesus Christ so that finite humans could try to comprehend the infinite on their own terms.

As an angel, I don't have to convince anyone of anything. But I do, at least, want people to think about why they believe what they do. I told you about the Creation, but I can't tell this story and leave the Messiah out; he is too intricately woven into the story.

Here's where discussions get interesting. How do you—or anyone—know that Jesus is the Messiah? Is it because he died on a cross? Two thieves died that day too—they don't get divine accolades. Lots of people died on crosses.[97] Humans devise crazy ways to hurt other humans. It's just odd. It is so strange that humans not only take the lives of others but also that they take the time to *think of ways* to take the lives of others. Humans really need to take up some more hobbies or reflect more on Philippians or something—but I digress. Anyway, this is where those first five books really come in handy.

Scripture is replete with G providing instructions on (1) how to love and (2) how to recognize the Messiah. The New Testament[98] is the good news. The thing that makes it good is that it heralds all the things the Old Testament was prophesying. It is as though in the Old Testament, G gives humans a giant gift all wrapped up, but humanity gets to open it in the New Testament.

The Messiah could not just appear without prophecy any more than a gift could magically appear on your doorstep. If a gift did suddenly appear, you may find yourself asking, *Is this for me? Where did this come from? What are we supposed to do with this? Who is this from, anyway?* Same with the Messiah. Every Tom, Dick, and Harry could claim to be the Messiah. G had to give very precise clues and

---

[97] I'm still not sure what humans have against the letter T that made it such an interesting form of torture. Eventually they branched out to the letter X, but the whole concept is baffling.

[98] Given the length of time it is actually out in public, it may be more appropriate to call it the "More Recent Testament" but that is a mouthful.

markers to make the true Messiah evident. By knowing Scripture, you would recognize the gift when it appeared. You would know who sent the gift and why it was offered. You got the gift in the Old Testament; you opened it via the New Testament. Ta-da! Now the only thing left is really filling out the thank-you card.

The Tree of Life tells you that you will get a gift, how you can recognize it, and what it means. G isn't being covert in providing the prophecies, but G is also not going to do all the work in the relationship. If G did all the work, it wouldn't be a relationship.

Imagine, if you will, a gentleman who is seeking a bride. This gentleman has so much to offer and wants to spend his life with someone who wants to be with him. Now this gentleman puts an ad in the local paper. He states that he likes pina coladas and getting caught in the rain. He wants a woman not into yoga who has half a brain. He then states that he will be at O'Malley's the next night[99] at seven, wearing a green tie.

A woman reads the ad and is intrigued. She wants to meet him. Now, you wouldn't expect her to show up and pour water on him, because it's not raining, and then produce copies of her EEG to provide ample evidence of cerebral functioning. If he gets offended, she can't cry out, "This is what you asked of me!" No, if she wants the relationship, she needs to spend time with him. She needs to learn that although he has provided general likes and dislikes, he has a bit more depth.

In fact, when she first walks in to meet him, she may not be able to pick him out among the men lingering at O'Malley's. How would she know him? Easy, he told her the time and place of his appearance. He also gave her some personal information so that he would be easily recognized. Now they can work on building a relationship, as she will have picked out the proper author of the ad.

It gets even better once she gets to know him. Once she gets to know him, she can pick him out whenever he is around. She will learn to recognize his voice, his behaviors, his likes, his dislikes, and his love. She will learn how to foster the relationship. At some point, the relationship may develop into an engagement.

---

[99] This would especially work if you wanted to date Rupert Holmes.

If she didn't read all of the advertisement, any man could come forward and claim to be the author. It is this way with G. G is inviting people into a relationship so that they will learn to recognize the voice and gifts and love of G when it is presented.

While there are many messianic prophecies scattered throughout Scripture, written centuries before the Messiah appeared, it is the five chapters of the Tree of Life that provides significant insight. Some of the greatest prophecies of the Messiah reveal themselves in the festivals G ordains.

G tells the people of Israel to celebrate seven specific festivals because they are "appointed feasts of the Lord that you shall proclaim as holy convocations." The Hebrew word used for "convocations" is *micrah*, which means "rehearsals." They are *rehearsals,* which means the final performance was yet to come! Of the seven festivals, six are annual events and the seventh is the weekly Sabbath. There are also monthly festivals, known as New Moon Festivals, which aren't technically Sabbaths but Pre-Exile had equal weight with the Sabbaths. The absence of the moon marked the first day of the month. It was critical to know the first day so you ensure proper timing of the other celebrations.[100] Paul defended these events, saying, "Let no one, then, pass judgment on you in matters of food and drink, or with regard to a festival or new moon or Sabbath. These are *shadows of things to come; the reality belongs to Christ.*"[101]

What does he mean by "shadows of things to come"? It sounds ominous and scary, or at the least, like a musing of Plato.[102] The truth is not scary at all and has nothing to do with shadows—well, maybe foreshadows … or seven shadows, as the case may be. In fact, it brings light when you understand what is going on. The festivals are the shadows. The Messiah is the one casting the shadows, the reality behind them.

---

[100] Check out Leviticus 23 for more insight. Just so you know, the Levites did not make jeans; that was the Levis.

[101] Paul got it! He even explained it in Colossians 2: 16–17.

[102] Not to be confused with Play-Doh, which is a-musing.

All of these festivals[103] prophesy the coming of the Christ. The rehearsals are performed over thousands of years, but they weren't your average, every day, run-of-the-mill parties. Whereby most parties just involve some music, Uriel grilling, or karaoke; these parties had rather quirky requirements.

Now, G wasn't trying to be bossy or controlling, but there was a point to each requirement. G was sending a message about how the Messiah would be born, die, come again—no, really, come again? Every step of every event was prophecy. Imagine if the macarena or the waltz was really some crazy, secret message about the grand scheme of life.[104] The party steps G provided were amazing because they were intricate, prophetic, and provided eons before their fruition. That's some pretty good accuracy. In fact, it is astounding, never-before-or-after-achieved accuracy by anyone other than G.

G loves a good gathering and figured this would be the most fun way to teach you how to expect the coming of Jesus and the second coming of Jesus and the first coming of John, aka the second coming of Elijah. That is why Paul says, when speaking of the rehearsals, "the reality belongs to Christ." The festivals are the rehearsals of the reality of Messiah.

The average Christian doesn't know the intricacies of the festivals celebrated by the Jewish people. Ironically enough, it is precisely those festivals that prove Jesus is the Messiah. The average Jewish person goes through the numerous rituals of the festivals,[105] not realizing that each step has just revealed the Messiah. The festivals are festivals now more than ever because the reality, the substance, the point behind them has been offered up.

How many Christians ask, *Why did John say Jesus was the Lamb of G?* How many Jewish people ask, *Why was a lamb killed to grant salvation?* Do they wonder collectively, does G have something against lambs? Nope. G loves animals. Perhaps it would be easier to just address the festivals and the messages behind each one to show how these reconcile.

---

[103] a.k.a. "rehearsal."

[104] What if the hokey-pokey was what it was really all about?

[105] To the extent possible ever since the destruction of the second temple.

SABBATONE[106]

Let's start with the weekly and the monthly festivals, the Sabbath, and the new moon festivals.

After creating the whole world and everything in it, including people, G took a break. Walking through the garden, admiring and enjoying creation, G called out to man and desired to spend time with him. Sabbath was a gift from G. G would supply all of man's needs, and all man had to do was rest and stop working long enough to have fellowship with G. Sabbath is the chance to catch up on old times, share a few laughs, and indulge in the beauty all around.

When man broke G's command not to eat from *the tree*, man chose a different ruler who would give him no rest, so you don't hear about Adam having weekends off, eight-hour days, or unions. He had no rest; he toiled. This is why the Sabbath is not mentioned in the Bible until the Israelites are delivered from Egypt during their mass exodus ... in Exodus. In leading the Israelites out of Egypt, G reclaimed them. In almost a mirror image of creation and salvation, G provided everything including saving the people from the evil one pursuing them. G provides them food, water, personal amenities, concierge services, and G gives them rest. You can imagine how much a day of no work meant to previous slaves.

As if spending the day chillin' with G was not the biggest perk of Sabbath, G promises a great many things for those who celebrate this weekly feast.[107] With such great rewards for simply kicking back, the natural question[108] must be, *How do I celebrate this feast?* The answer is really quite simple—do not work. Rest. So when the Sabbath rolls around, kick back in a hammock, love, laugh, spend time with G and creation. Stop attempting to create or build up worldly houses or wealth and build instead on the immortal. Do your spiritual weightlifting.[109]

---

[106] The sound of several Sabbaths.

[107] Check out my man Isaiah for more insight on this one—Isaiah 56:2–8; 58:13 to name a few.

[108] After, "How did I get to be so lucky?"

[109] FYI—The one thing in your house that should never be dusty is your Bible.

The Sabbath reveals what life will be like in the kingdom. Do you want to know what you will do after you die? Look at what you do on the Sabbath. You should engage in fellowship with G, commune with others, relax, and have minimal Brussels sprouts.[110]

The monthly celebrations are a bit different. After the Hebrews were freed from the Egyptians, one of the first orders of business was to shift to the lunar calendar—a 180-degree turn from the solar calendar of the Egyptians. The lunar calendar would be a tool for the Jewish people to set their times, holidays, and seasons. Knowing the start of the months is critical in order to calibrate—and celebrate—the festivals properly. It also served philosophical purposes, mirroring the creation story, whereby the person would move from the darkness and into the light as a sign of deliverance. The monthly new-moon celebrations are called *Rosh Chodesh*, "head of the month," and were associated with rebirth.

Depending on when the new moon falls in relation to a Sabbath, differing scriptures are read. If the new moon falls on the Sabbath, the last chapter of the book of Isaiah is read. That scripture is interesting as it speaks directly of the Messiah and how during the Messiah's reign "from new moon to new moon, and from Sabbath to Sabbath, all flesh shall come to worship before me." The key here is that all will come, not just the chosen ones.[111] Jesus pointed out that *all* will be called and all must be reborn—not of the body, but of the heart.

In the Gospels you hear of how a holy man named Nicodemus came to Jesus in the dark of the night and has what may, on its face, appear a confusing conversation. Nicodemus gives Jesus a nice compliment and states that he believes Jesus has come from G.

Jesus responds, "Very truly I tell you, no one can see the kingdom of G unless they are born again." Many people may pause on this remark and wonder if Jesus was actually listening to what Nick had just said. A human's first response may be something like "Dude, he just paid you a compliment, and you are yapping about rebirth. And why are you guys running around in the dark night?"

---

[110] I made up that last part.

[111] The Jewish people are known as the "chosen ones" but G loves and calls everyone.

Nick responds, "How can someone be born when they are old? Surely, they cannot enter a second time into their mother's womb." If you don't understand the context of the remarks, you may feel as if you just walked in on an inside joke.

If you consider *when* the remarks were made—in the dark of night—it would shed some light on the situation. Ha-ha. This isn't just any night; it is Rosh Chodesh. Rosh Chodesh was and is equated with rebirth. Recall that these men would have heard scripture this day on rebirth and the Messiah. Nick just mentioned to Jesus how he believes Jesus is from G. Jesus then refers to the rebirth that the Messiah would usher in. Now, for the average Jewish person, being born into Judaism is all that is required to call yourself a Jew. If your parents are Jewish, you don't have to undergo anything above and beyond what other Jewish people undergo. You have a birthright. If you were not born Jewish and you wanted to become Jewish, you had to undergo certain rites to be "born into" the faith.

Nick believes that since he is born Jewish, there is nothing more to be born into. The rebirth would be reserved for Gentiles or other people converting into Judaism, but not the Jews themselves. This is where Jesus points out that the rebirth must occur within *every* heart. Every person must be born again from darkness into the light, just as the festival commemorates. This is to what Jesus refers when he talks to Nick.

ANNUAL FESTIVITIES

The six *annual* events are grouped by season: three in the spring and three in the fall.[112] The spring festivals—Passover, Firstfruits of the Barley Harvest, and Shavuot[113]—have already happened, not in the seasonal sense but in the fulfillment-of-prophecy sense. The fall festival of Sukkot has occurred. Rosh Hashana, and Yom Kippur foreshadow[114] what will happen in the future, but hasn't

---

[112] Two seasons, two comings of the Messiah.

[113] Also known as Pentecost.

[114] "Twoshadow" would be a more accurate term.

actually occurred in the grand-finale sense. And this time, I got the chronology right.

Let's start with a general overview of the spring festivals. I am going to give you just the high-level comparisons; for a full-blown theological review, you should actually study Scripture. After all, you can't rely on any one person to do the entire relationship building, angel or not. The spring festival of Passover foreshadows the death of the Messiah. The festival of Firstfruits of the Barley Harvest foreshadows the resurrection of the Messiah, and G's Holy Spirit consecrating the new covenant is foreshadowed in Shavuot.

G said in the book of Deuteronomy that the festivals that G requests are "rehearsals of things to come." As I mentioned earlier, at some point people need to pause and reflect on what they are rehearsing and why. What could they possibly be rehearsing?[115] The real events to come!

PASSOVER—DEATH OF THE LAMB

Let's start with Passover. The initial Passover began with a sacrifice of a spotless lamb preceding deliverance from death and an evil ruler. Thereafter, Passover celebrated the deliverance from bondage, but the rite of celebration still involved the sacrifice of a lamb without defect.

What kind of rehearsal would have G asking for the death of a lamb? Hmm. Maybe the death of the Lamb? The first thing John the Baptist said of Jesus was "Behold! The Lamb of G!" Why would John call him that? Why? Because John was pointing out that the lamb sacrifice of Passover was intended to foreshadow the death of the Messiah.

The Passover celebration started a long time ago as a remembrance of the past salvation of the Israelites from Pharaoh during the exodus. Perhaps some context would be in order here. The Hebrews went to Egypt during a great famine when Joseph, one of their own, was second only to Pharaoh. They were treated well when they first got there. Through time and administration changes, new powers

---

[115] Insert theme to *Jeopardy* here.

and pressures came into play, and those powers feared the Hebrews. The Hebrews were forced into slavery. A Hebrew named Moses, who, through a weird turn of events, was raised by Pharaoh's daughter, came to know G. In fact, G selected Moses to free the Hebrews from the Egyptians.

Moses agreed and asked Pharaoh for permission for the Hebrew slaves to spend three days in the desert worshiping G. Being a stubborn ruler, Pharaoh said no. It's a pretty phenomenal story in and of itself. Many people wonder why G didn't just swoop in and smite Pharaoh. Why would G? Pharaoh was just a man. It is one thing when the Almighty G comes after you personally; it's another thing to be beaten by an old man who used to be a slave. Talk about a lesson in humility.

We are talking a shutout of epic proportions. Pharaoh believed he was a god, so G used a man to defeat him.

Moses' first humble request, to let the Hebrews go to worship G, was presented with an impressive staff-turned-to-serpent trick. Seriously, Moses dropped his staff and it turned into a snake. Keep in mind that the snake was highly revered by the Egyptians. Taunting the Egyptians with a snake was tantamount to taunting a Rottweiler with a T-bone. Pharaoh yelled, "Come at me, Bro!" and had his advisors come for the staff meeting. The advisors turned their staffs into snakes. Moses' snake, much like a contestant on *Fear Factor*, gobbled up all of Pharaoh's snakes.[116] After indulging in an all-you-can-eat snake buffet, Moses' snake returned to a staff—a fuller, fatter staff,[117] but a staff nonetheless.

Pharaoh pretty much challenged Moses and said, "Game on." Moses, together with his sidekick/brother Aaron, acted as a catalyst for a series of plagues. The plagues started with the most critical and fundamental element in all of Egypt—the Nile. G had the brothers turn it to blood. It was a very impressive show, something you might see in Vegas … or not. It certainly got the attention of Pharaoh, and of hemophiliacs. Keep in mind, the Egyptians believed that the Nile had its own god. Moses not only brought Pharaoh down a notch,

---

[116] You could say he had a staff infection.

[117] It had been months since his staff had last eaten.

but he totally discredited any argument that the Nile had any divine overseer aside from G.

The plagues then gradually evolved from the water to the land and into the air. So after blood, it was frogs[118] that plagued the Egyptians. Next came gnats—they were very gannoying.

After gnats, flies[119] plagued the Egyptians. Not only did the plagues slowly elevate, they also got bigger. After flies, the livestock was struck dead (then they were dead-stock).

Tormenting the cattle didn't seem to impress Pharaoh. Some people believe that G forced Pharaoh to be obstinate, because several times throughout Scripture G states, "I will harden Pharaoh's heart." This statement is akin to "Now I am really going to tick him off." You aren't forcing someone to be mad, but you know that person well enough to know his reaction. G knows people, inside and out.

So the plagues have increased from the water (blood), to land and water (frogs), to low-elevation gannoyances (gnats), to higher-elevation pests (flies), to big animals, and now humans will be hit. The next plague was boils (but they occurred at ambient air temperature, not 212 degrees Fahrenheit). Still Pharaoh was obstinate. Losing the slaves would mean the Egyptians would actually have to build their own buildings, cook their own food, do their own dishes, and get up to change the television station because remote controls were not yet invented.

As Pharaoh gave no relief, G then elevated the plagues yet again. Now the plague came from the sky; hail was going to fall. As he had done with all the plagues, Moses gave the Egyptians a big head's up. Interestingly enough, some Egyptians started paying attention to Moses. Even some of Pharaoh's officials listened to the words Moses spoke and brought their animals and slaves in from the fields lest they die. Well, all hail broke loose. Any animals or people out in the fields died. The crops died (aka dead crops), and the trees were stripped. Nobody likes naked trees.

---

[118] A fact only to be appreciated by puppet female pigs and hungry Frenchmen.

[119] Do you know what you call a fly without wings? A walk.

As in some bad horror-movie episode,[120] Pharaoh still didn't learn. He just couldn't figure it out. He again backed out on his promise to let the Hebrews go to worship G. Now the plague came from the sky, but instead of a cold, lifeless plague from above, this plague lived. Any plant or crop not destroyed by the hail was ravaged by the locusts—which are a lot like angry flies on steroids.

When Pharaoh backed down yet again on releasing the captives, the next plague was from the very heavens themselves—darkness. Keep in mind, the Egyptians didn't have flashlights, and it's hard to start a fire when you can't find the kindling. Total and complete darkness covered all the areas of Egypt, but it did not affect the areas inhabited by the Hebrews. G was making a point here: those who turn from G may find themselves lost in darkness. The Hebrews may have been slaves, but they were having a better time than the taskmasters at this point. After darkness so complete you could almost feel it, the next plague will be the last; and you know how grand finales can be.

It is this last plague that prompts the Passover festival. G told Moses that during the night the firstborn sons of Egypt would die. There is a strange irony here. Moses was raised by Pharaoh's daughter. He was raised by Pharaoh's daughter because during Moses' infancy, the reigning Pharaoh ordered that the male Hebrew children be killed. Now the male child who miraculously escaped the edict of death from Pharaoh was looking at Pharaoh telling him the firstborn males would die. The irony is for you to explore; I will go back to my story.

The angel of death would be released and would claim the firstborn son of everyone, but the angel would pass over[121] the house of anyone who performed in accordance with G's instructions. Naturally, G gave pretty explicit instructions on what to do. The reason is twofold. First, each step performed during the Passover also foreshadowed the sacrifice of the Lamb of G, the Messiah. G was giving prophecy;

---

[120] You know those episodes—when the characters hear a strange, scary noise and instead of calling for help or grabbing a weapon, they go walking in the darkness with a failing flashlight to investigate.

[121] Hence the name Passover. Think about it—if the angel had gone a different direction, the festival could be called "Passunder" or "Go Around."

that G, always thinking. Second, while the steps generally seem quite benign, anyone who was willing to do them heralded their faith in G. Scripture recounts many instances whereby G asks someone to do something counterintuitive,[122] or counterclockwise or not intuitive, but G does the miracle; humans show the faith.[123]

The most prominent requirement of the Passover was to kill a lamb, dip some hyssop in the blood, and put the blood on the top and sides of the doorframe. It sounds quite odd, but it does make the believers in G rather easy to identify. It's not like someone would have accidentally done this; if you have hyssop-scented blood on your doorframe, it's safe to say you were listening to G's instructions.

Terror struck. The firstborn of everyone and everything not in a house shielded by the blood of the lamb died. Pharaoh relented. The Israelites were free to leave for three days to worship G in the wilderness.

Moses and the people collected the bones of Joseph[124] and began their journey. The first night they camped at the edge of the desert. By the second day, Pharaoh heard that the Israelites were escaping, so he changed his mind about giving them three days, chased after the Israelites, and caught up to them on the second night. But very early on the third morning, Moses tells his people to stand firm and they would see the salvation (the actual word used was *Yeshua*, which is, intentionally enough, also the Hebrew pronunciation of the name Jesus) the Lord will bring them.

This is also a most wonderful area of Scripture for learning how to deal with the spiritual battles you humans face. Moses sums up the proper response to spiritual attacks in one sentence: "The Lord will fight for you; you need only to be still." People often follow the will of G, but then panic when they see an enemy or a threat. Humans

---

[122] A good example of this is Joshua walking around the city of Jericho to make the walls fall. Who would have thunk it?

[123] Like the old saying goes "You do everything possible; G will do the impossible."

[124] Joseph had actually requested before he died that his bones be taken out of Egypt when the Jews left; they weren't hoarders or anything like that. But it is important to note that *Joseph's tomb was empty.*

can be like Peter who walks on water in faith but sinks when he takes his eyes off his Yeshua[125] and focuses on the storm around him. Take your eyes off your salvation and you'll struggle.

The Israelites don't have to raise a single fist or weapon. Moses parts the Red Sea, allowing the Israelites to cross over to safety. The Egyptians who followed behind them are swallowed by the sea.

Well, now you have a general overview as to what prompted the Passover. I hear people say all the time that "hindsight is 20/20," which does not mean much if time is all the same and you struggle with chronology, like yours truly, but people do seem a lot better at understanding things when they have already happened. The Israelites correctly understood that Passover was celebrating their salvation; the problem is the mistaken belief that the festival is limited only to *past* salvation. G clearly stated in Deuteronomy that these festivals were rehearsals of things *to come*, not just of things that *were*. This makes even more sense when you contemplate the festivals in concert with Ecclesiastes 1:9: "What has been will be again, what has been done will be done again; there is nothing new under the sun." G saved the people from the rule of the evil one. That which has been done will be done again.

Passover requires the people to get a lamb without blemish.[126] To make sure that this directive was honored in its fullness, the more devout households would choose a lamb without blemish on the tenth day of Nisan.[127] They would inspect the lamb for a few days to make sure that the lamb was indeed without blemish and that it didn't get blemished before the appointed time.

An interesting little side point here is that the lambs that were reserved for the temple sacrifice were raised in a small town called Nazareth; as was Jesus. The lambs would be paraded into Jerusalem on the tenth day of the month, and throngs of people would gather along the road to watch sheep on parade.[128] Visitors to the city

---

[125] A.k.a Jesus, a.k.a. Salvation

[126] See Exodus 12 for more insight on this.

[127] No relation to the car.

[128] Kind of like the things you see on television around Thanksgiving but without the large floats and annoying announcers.

would also join in the parade. The people would wave palms and sing praises, specifically psalms[129] endearingly called the Hallel.[130] The psalms that were sung related directly to the coming Messiah. Jesus was selected by his people as the lamb without blemish; so much so that he was placed on a donkey and joined the parade into Jerusalem on the same day. As he rode, he would have been listening to the crowd sing the songs—or psalms—of the Messiah. "Blessed is he who comes in the name of the Lord!"

Jesus goes into the city again on the eleventh, twelfth, and part of the thirteenth to be examined. While the devout Jews inspected their lamb, the leaders and teachers of the law inspected Jesus; he stumped the Sadducees[131] and the Pharisees.[132] He sailed through their traps without stumbling and emerged from their cross-examinations completely unscathed. He eventually came before Pontius Pilate and King Herod. Pilate remarked that he could find no fault with Jesus. Just like the priests rendering a lamb without defect and worthy of sacrifice—Pilate did the same. Herod also found no fault—I guess that makes him a co-Pilate.

On the thirteenth of Nisan, Jesus has a Passover Seder with his disciples. Granted, Jesus had his Seder the night before the Seder was ordained. This was necessary because he would be living out the real Passover on the ordained night. By having the Seder with his disciples on the evening before the real event, he was able to point out that he was, in fact, the Lamb of G, the star of the Passover show.

Jesus even pointed out the correlation, as while he was eating Passover, he told his disciples to "do this in memory of me." This didn't mean that every time you eat bread or drink wine, you should remember the Messiah—although that isn't a bad idea by any stretch of the imagination. Jesus was pointing out that when you eat and drink at the Passover, you are in fact rehearsing his death. It is the prophecy of his death unfolding. It is the memorial of the Messiah.

---

[129] The confused people would wave psalms and sing palms.

[130] See Psalms 113–118, and revel in the amazing Messianic foreshadowing therein. As Jesus rode into town, those words were spoken around him, to him.

[131] They were sad-you-see.

[132] Actually, they were not-so-fair-you-see.

Prior to Pilate condemning Jesus to the cross, he pointed out that due to the special occasion, a prisoner could be released. The people could choose between a murderer, named Barabbas, or Jesus. The Hebrew translation of *Barabbas* means "son of the father." The people had to choose either the one *named* the son of the father or the one *deemed* the Son of the Father. They, like Adam, turned their back on the real G in favor of the artificial one.

On the fourteenth day of Nisan, Jesus was taken to Golgotha, also known as The Skull, to be crucified. The large stones removed during the construction of the temple were discarded at Golgotha and gave the appearance of a skull. Jesus, rejected, was on the cross surrounded by the stones rejected in the building of the temple. Interestingly enough, throughout the centuries of Passover celebrations, it was customary for the priests also to sing the Hallel during the Passover sacrifice. During Jesus' time on the cross he would have heard in the background the singing of Psalm 118, which includes the line "The stone that the builders rejected became the capstone."

Prior to and eons after the death of the Messiah, in some parts of the world when the lamb for the Passover meal is cooked, the lamb is stood upright, with a rod inserted up through the middle of the lamb and a rod placed across the rib cage. In essence, the animal is cooked on a cross. The entrails are wrapped around the lamb's head while it is cooked upright. If you squint your eyes when looking at the lamb, it looks like a man on a cross with thorns around his head.

Up until the time of the scheduled execution, displaying the lamb was the next step in the Passover festival. Jesus was on display until his death. He drew a huge crowd as he carried the cross and then was hung on it for the whole city to see.

When Jesus was hung on the cross, the words "Jesus of Nazareth, King of the Jews" were hung over his head. The Pharisees tried to have Pilate alter the sign to read "*He claimed* he was King of the Jews." Pilate refused.

Jesus was hung between two thieves, one of whom taunted Jesus. But the second thief rebuked the other, saying, "Don't you fear G, since you are under the same sentence? We are punished justly, for we are getting what our deeds deserve. But this man has done nothing wrong." The contrite thief then said to Jesus, "Remember me when you come into your kingdom."

Two men stand before the Tree of the Knowledge of Good and Evil and the Tree of Life. Even in their final hours, they have the ability to choose. One man continues in his pride. The other man pauses and reflects on his life, his actions, his punishment, and also the state of the innocent man beside him. Notice how compassion falls from his lips. In the midst of his personal suffering and, by his own admission, his deserved, excruciating punishment—he thinks about someone else—Jesus. That thief was able to recognize two absolutely critical principles of life. First, he sinned by his own choice. No one made him sin; no one forced his hand. Second, sin cannot defeat you. It can make you feel guilty, proud, insecure, and a great many other things, but it can always be overcome. The atonement was being made. Through compassion and humility, the thief was able to see exactly who Jesus was. He said, "*Your* kingdom." The last kind words said to the Messiah were said by an outcast of society.

Jesus informed the criminal, "Truly I tell you, today you will be with me in paradise." There were no formalities that had to be employed. There were no legalistic mandates, no rites of passage, no sacrifices, no other actions this thief had to perform in order to see paradise. He simply turned to Christ with a sincere and repentant heart.

Next Jesus said, "My G, my G, why have thou forsaken me?" Most people think that Jesus was mad at G. Not the case. Jesus was reciting Psalm 22. See, in those days, these days, the days that are during this time, Scripture wasn't parsed into numbers. Jesus couldn't yell out, "Look! I'm fulfilling Psalm 22!" because it wasn't actually numbered yet, but the people who knew Scripture knew to what he was referring.

Psalm 22 was written by King David, and it speaks about how his hands and feet are pierced, how they cast lots for his clothes—all things that happened to the Messiah but never happened to David. People used to wonder what David was talking about when he made the comments, because the events about which David wrote didn't all happen to him. If you had read the psalm before Jesus came on the scene, you would have scratched your head and said, "Um, David, aren't you exaggerating just a bit on how bad your situation really is?" To which he would have held up his hand and said, "Talk to the Messiah."

Originally, the Jewish people had two major views about the prophesied Messiah. Some believed the Messiah would resemble David, others Joseph; the distinctions were dubbed Messiah ben David or Messiah ben Joseph. It mighta ben (*chuckle*) helpful if the two parties realized there was a way to reconcile their positions, as they were not mutually exclusive. See, on one hand,[133] David was a powerful king. A lot of Jews were waiting for the Messiah to be a earthly, physical king—like David. While Jesus was a king like David, his kingdom was not of this world.[134]

On the other hand,[135] Joseph (with his amazing Technicolor dream coat) was a man who suffered before being appointed second in command. Joseph was a picture of the Messiah. See, Joseph was sold into slavery by his own brothers for some silver. He was thrown into a pit, he was put into prison in Egypt, but then he was raised up and became powerful, second only to Pharaoh. People called him the bread man of life, and he was given a non-Jew (also known as a Gentile[136]) for a bride. In a similar way, Jesus was handed over by his brothers; one in particular sold him out for money. Jesus died and was buried, but then he rose again as second in command to G. Jesus, the Jew, took in the Gentiles with great love, to the point of calling them his bride, and was known as the Bread of Life.

So some Jews thought the Messiah would rule à la King David, and others believe he would suffer à la Joseph. Prophecy supported both positions. Funny thing is—they both were right. In Jesus' first coming, he was more akin to Messiah ben Joseph. In his second coming, he will align with the Messiah ben David.

Jesus then cried out, "Father, into your hands I commit my spirit." Remember earlier how I told you that Jesus was pointing out how he

---

[133] You have five fingers.

[134] Jesus even mentioned this to Pilate in one of their conversations.

[135] You have five more fingers!

[136] Although they weren't always gentle.

was fulfilling Psalm 22 by his cry from the cross? Well, now Jesus is quoting Psalm 31,[137] another prophetic psalm of David's. At three in the afternoon, on the fourteenth day of Nisan, at the exact time the Passover lambs were being slaughtered, Jesus breathed his last breath and died.

He was buried late that day,[138] and we hear no more for three nights.[139] This part gets confusing for a lot of people. They think Jesus was in the tomb for two nights. This is an easy mistake to make if you are not Jewish. The Jewish days mirror the creation; they begin at sunset, not sunrise. Jesus was put into the tomb just *before* sunset starting the Friday. (This would have been *Thursday* night for non-Jews, the start of Friday for Jews.) So Jesus first went into the tomb on the first night. That night and following day was a Sabbath as the Jewish people were eating their Passover lambs. Then the second night fell. (This is *Friday* night for non-Jews, the start of Saturday for the Jews.) Saturdays are the weekly Sabbath for the Jewish people; therefore, no burying or anointing the dead was allowed. Then the third night fell. (This is *Saturday* night for non-Jews, the start of Sunday for the Jews.) Jesus' followers couldn't go into the dark tomb to anoint him at night. They had to wait until daylight. Sunday morning, Jesus rose from the dead.[140]

For centuries, the Jews indulged in the festivities of Passover and knew the history behind all the symbols. But there was a problem in understanding the prophecy of each symbol; primarily, how could a human possibly be a lamb offering? When Abraham took Isaac up to the mountain in order to sacrifice him, he was questioned by his son, who said, "Where is the lamb for the sacrifice?" Abraham stated that "G would provide the sacrifice." And G would. G provided G's Son as a sacrifice so humans would stop sacrificing one another

---

[137] Give this psalm a gander to get a better feel for the prophetic nature of the verse.

[138] Interestingly enough, Jesus was put into the tomb of Joseph of Arimathea. Upon his resurrection, and much like the exodus from Egypt, Joseph's tomb was empty.

[139] Check out Matthew 12:40

[140] If you are Jewish, you are probably nodding and saying "I get it. Move on." If you are not Jewish, you may be waiting for me to break into an Abbott and Costello routine. Don't get hung up on it.

on battlefields, in domestic quarrels, and in war. G provided the sacrifice for all humanity so that no other sacrifices would need to be made. Ancient *Midrash*[141] recognizes that G would provide an eternal sacrifice, as the sacrifice of animals was only temporary. In fact, Jewish people could only sacrifice at the Temple. Shortly after Jesus died, the Temple was destroyed and the ability to continue with animal sacrifices ceased.

When time came for the sacrifice of Isaac, Abraham was stopped by divine intervention. Then he saw a *ram* in the *distance*. Funny thing about translations, the passage that mentions that bit can also be translated to say that Abraham saw the *salvation* in the *future*. This would be corroborated by Jesus, who flatly stated that Abraham rejoiced to see his day.

G created the festival of Passover—so familiar to a people who love celebrations—to prepare them for the real, main-stage event. Some people were unable to look beyond the surface and see that Jesus played the role perfectly, bringing into the present the fulfillment of the historical celebration. Passover represented not only freedom from slavery but freedom from sin and the consequence of death. Jesus was the Passover lamb and fulfilled the festival in his person, setting all people free.

This last part about setting people free often baffles people. They don't get what it means when someone says, "Jesus died for you." They scratch their heads and say, "Well, I didn't ask him to." Here's the deal: G doesn't lie. G doesn't renege on promises, deals, or arrangements. G gave Adam and Eve a garden and pretty much said that if they decided to sin, the penalty of sin was death. Think of it as a penalty clause in a contract. Well, Adam and Eve sinned. They died. Sin equals death. This is where Lucifer steps in. If he can encourage people to sin, he can ensure their death. However, Jesus didn't sin. He could have. He had the free will to do so if he chose; but he didn't. He was innocent. Lucifer intervened. Lucifer encouraged Jesus' killing. Jesus was killed. Now all bets were off. The agreement

---

[141] A compilation of ancient Hebrew books to help explain the Scripture. It is not a skin disorder.

was sin equals death. Innocence did not equal death. The contract was broken when an innocent man was killed.

You can look at this from two ways. One, Jesus had the contract invalidated. He took on all the world's sins, so now anyone who wanted to be redeemed could point to the Redeemer and say, "Hey, Lucifer, *you* broke the agreement! Deal's off, I'm with him. You can't lay claim to me." Or two, it's simply a whole new ball game. Either option works.

Let me tell you a story to illustrate my point. A father took his child camping in the woods one weekend. After a fun-filled morning of playing, the family returned to their campsite. They decided to rest in the tent for a little bit. The father awoke to discover his young child had wandered away. In a panic, he began searching around the campsite. He couldn't find the young child. He flagged down a park ranger who called in a search team. Hours passed. The child was not to be found.

The father, so desperate to see his child, fell on his knees. He cried out to G "Take my money. Take my job. Take *my life* instead of my child's. I will give everything I have if only my child would come home safe."

When humans are on earth, they are on a trip with G away from the true home. Humans will wander away from G. Jesus knew he would be wrongly killed, but he also knew that if he was killed, all of his children could be brought home safely because the deal would be off. With the same love of a father desperate to find his child, Jesus humbly gave up his life so that he can embrace his wandering children when they finally make it home.

Everything Jesus did fulfilled prophecies of one kind or another, but so much has been lost in society through the dilution of the festivals. The Jewish people have the prophetic festivals but failed to appreciate the symbolism of their actions. The Christians have man-made holidays devoid of prophecy, but they have the fulfillment of the prophecy they don't know. One religion has the question, the other has the answer. The two should really get together and talk more.

All the holidays G ordained have significance. You know, in this discussion of religious festivals, I should make a few side points.

Many people accuse the Jewish of becoming too legalistic. They took a few short books of G's simple commands and turned them into volumes upon volumes of ritualistic requirements. This is true. In the attempt to build protective fences around the rules of G, they created so many regulations that they burden men down. Jesus himself called out this shortcoming ... or very "longcoming," depending on how you look at it.

Overregulation has led Christians to throw out all Jewish rituals entirely. Some Christians have gone so far as to dispose of all the Old Testament except random provisions that are arbitrarily deemed worthy of keeping.[142] Weirdly enough, many of these same Christians who denounce Old Testament rules because they come under the "law" have established holidays and mandatory "holy days of obligation" that have no scriptural basis.

Now, G isn't looking for pure law followers, or else people would become like the older brother in Jesus' parable or the Pharisees who keep the laws and lack compassion. But G also doesn't seek complete disregard of the Word, either, or else people will subjectively begin defining morality and using that as justification for when to mete out or withhold compassion.[143]

One side reads Scripture and interprets the requirements to the highest, most conservative level; the other group entirely dismisses significant portions of Scripture and establishes an entirely independent framework for worship. The correct answer is in between these dichotomies. Read the Scripture, which, yes, includes the Old Testament. Don't add to the requirements, and don't take away from them. If you are confused, pray. Seek wisdom. Don't make more rules, and don't ignore the ones you don't like. When in doubt, pray.

FIRSTFRUITS OF THE BARLEY HARVEST—RESURRECTION

So three days after Jesus died, it was the seventeenth of Nisan. Early in the morning, Mary Magdalene went to the tomb and found

---

[142] The Ten Commandments are often retained.

[143] Even Paul called out the need to examine a prophet's words against Scripture. During Paul's time, the New Testament wasn't complete.

it empty. Jesus had risen; death was overcome. The seventeenth of Nisan repeatedly proved to be a day of salvation for the Jewish. It was the day that the ark came to rest on Mt. Ararat.[144] The day marks the day the Israelites were delivered out of the sea when being chased by Pharaoh.[145] It was the day Esther was able to save her people from Haman, a nasty man who tried to have the Jews killed.[146] It was the day the Israelites ate the food of the Promised Land.[147] And it was the day that Jesus rose from the dead.

Well, three days after the prophetic Passover is the second spring-fling, prophetic celebration called the Firstfruits of the Barley Harvest—or FFBH for the slow of tongue. Say that ten times fast. Then do a little dance.[148] A harvest in Scripture generally represents the separating and calling of those who put their faith in the Messiah.[149] This particular harvest is specific to barley, which was the first grain to ripen. Barley is a coarse grain, so much so that the rich people didn't eat it.[150] The rich ate wheat, leaving barley for poor people and animals.

Because barley ripens before the other grains, it was not likely that people would eat other grains during the time barley sacrifices were offered, but nonetheless, the firstfruits of the barley harvest had to be offered before the rest of the grains were fit to eat. It was tithing at its finest. It was giving the first of the blessing back to the one who blessed.

During the Passover services, a gaggle of priests crossed a bridge over the Kidron Valley, which was known to the locals as the valley of the shadow of death,[151] to a plot of land on the Mount of Olives

---

[144] Genesis 8:4

[145] Exodus 3:18; 5:3, 14

[146] Esther 3:1–6

[147] Joshua 5:1–12

[148] Make a little love, get down tonight.

[149] Matthew 13:39; Mark 4:26–29; Luke 10:1–12

[150] Many in history will grow to love drinking it, however.

[151] It was aptly called this as the remains from the sacrifices were discarded there, so it was full of bones and creepy, smelly things. The priests had to cross by bridge or they would make themselves unclean and never get the stains off their robes.

dedicated to growing barley.¹⁵² At the garden, the priests bound sheaths of barley but did not cut it down until after the Sabbath. After the Sabbath, a crowd gathered to watch the ceremony. Three priests cut down three ephahs of barley and placed it in three baskets.¹⁵³ The barley was gathered and carried back to the temple, where it would be winnowed, roasted, and ground. A tenth of the barley (an omer¹⁵⁴) was passed through thirteen¹⁵⁵ sieves to make it a pure offering. This process made the resulting flour so fine that it met or exceeded the finest wheat flour.

So, where is the Messiah in this picture? First of all, Paul flat-out states that Jesus is the Firstfruits. Paul stated in 1 Corinthians¹⁵⁶ "But Christ has indeed been raised from the dead, the *firstfruits* of those that have fallen asleep. For since death came through a man, the resurrection of the dead comes also through a man. For as in Adam all die, so in Christ all will be made alive. But each in turn: Christ, *the firstfruits*; then, when he comes, those who belong to him."

Second, just as barley did not win a popularity contest, so too did Jesus lose in that area. Jesus drew crowds in some of the places he visited, but in his hometown people rejected him and even wanted to kill him. Isaiah describes the Messiah well when he says, "He had no beauty or majesty to attract us to him, nothing in his appearance that we should desire him."

Third, Jesus served the poor, just as barley was served to the poor. Jesus was unpopular, unwanted, and the first to truly open up the way for others. Jesus' ministry embraced the poor. Matthew tells of the time when Jesus went into the synagogue and read the words of Isaiah: "'The Spirit of the Lord is on me, because he has anointed

---

¹⁵² The name suggests that growing olives, but the Mount of Barley didn't sound as cool.

¹⁵³ There's that number 3 again.

¹⁵⁴ No relation to Bart Simpson's dad.

¹⁵⁵ Thirteen is not an unlucky number. When G passed before Moses, thirteen distinct qualities were used to describe G. There were twelve tribes of Israel plus the tribe of Levi. There were twelve disciples plus one for Jesus. There are thirteen doughnuts in a baker's dozen. Lots of good things associated with thirteen.

¹⁵⁶ But *to* lots of Corinthians …

me to proclaim good news to the poor. He has sent me to proclaim freedom for the prisoners and recovery of sight for the blind, to set the oppressed free, to proclaim the year of the Lord's favor.' Then he rolled up the scroll, gave it back to the attendant and sat down. The eyes of everyone in the synagogue were fastened on him. He began by saying to them, 'Today this scripture is fulfilled in your hearing.'"

He ate with the poor, the thieves, and the commoners. He blessed the poor; he ministered to the poor. Often the poor were seen as cursed by G. The demoralizing of the poor made it hard for them to overcome their circumstances.

Jesus pointed out that the poor were not poor because of a curse or lack of compassion on G's part but from a lack of compassion on the part of other people. G gave enough for everyone; when people choose to hoard or not share, it is not G's will. Poverty is failure on the part of the rich. G never said to hoard goods or store up assets. Jesus specifically warns against storing up earthly treasures that moths destroy and thieves may steal. Whether you want it to happen or not, everything you have will be taken from you at some point in time. By giving it away while you are still alive, you can at least experience the beauty and joy of giving.

Fourth, like the barley, Jesus was cut down in his prime. When the priests were carrying the barley back to the temple on the seventeenth of Nisan, Jesus was crossing over a proverbial valley of the shadow of death to return to the holy—the holiest—of places.

By the end of the ceremony, the quality of coarse barley exceeded that of the finest grains. This day began with Jesus in a tomb and ended with him being glorified.

Remember the story of the rich man and the beggar named Lazarus? In case it doesn't jump to your recollection, let me help.

There was a rich guy who had a pretty swanky place to live, and there was a beggar named Lazarus at his gate. The fact that the beggar was at his gate meant Lazarus saw the man quite frequently. Anyway, the beggar died and was carried to Abraham's side. The rich man died too. He wasn't as fortunate. He ended up in a much hotter place.

The rich man sees Lazarus resting comfortably in the company of Abraham and calls to Abraham to have the beggar bring him some water,[157] as he was in agony and needed some relief. Abraham pointed out that there was a time when the rich man had good things and Lazarus did not. Now the tables were turned. Besides, there was a chasm between them, and Lazarus could not cross over.

Then the rich man asked if Abraham would send Lazarus to his brothers to warn them of the fate that awaited the selfish.[158]

Abraham again declines—pointing out that the rich man's brothers had Moses and the prophets. The rich man persists, claiming that if someone from the dead goes to them, they will repent. Abraham correctly, and quite prophetically, points out that if they will not listen to the prophets, "they will not be convinced even if someone rises from the dead."[159]

As someone without a sense of chronology, I could never understand the confusion around the story of Lazarus. People ask why Lazarus was with Abraham after death, and not with G. I can hardly resist correcting them by using the present tense and giving an affirmative response for both: Lazarus is with Abraham, and both are with G. Instead I tilt my head slightly, place my index finger on my chin, and with a most scholarly demeanor reply that like the other grains in the harvest that cannot be eaten until the barley sacrifice has been offered, Lazarus and the righteous could not enter heaven until Jesus was first raised from the dead. Matthew corroborates my story by pointing out that after Jesus' resurrection, the tombs were opened and the righteous traveled to the holy city. The firstfruit was offered, so the rest of the harvest is fit and can enter the kingdom.

The FFBH has morphed over time. The celebration for the Jewish people continues as a festival involving grain tithing. The celebration has been mutated by Christians, who will come to call it Easter, and lacks all the foreshadowing and prophecy of the original FFBH celebrations. Don't get me wrong—any celebration of the Messiah is good; it's just that the Christian customs can be rather arbitrary.

---

[157] Interesting how the rich man wouldn't just ask Lazarus himself. Then again, he spent so many years ignoring the man that it would be quite humbling to talk to him now.

[158] How entitled is this man? Even in hell, he seeks to have Lazarus do his bidding.

[159] This statement is pregnant with foreshadowing.

FFBH offers an exceptional segue into the next holiday. FFBH kicks off the minor festival called the counting of the omer. This is a counting of the days until the next major celebration. There will be fifty days between the two festivals.

SHAVUOT/PENTECOST—BETROTHAL

Because of the fifty-day nuance, the next festival is called Pentecost, because that literally means "fifty days." This is the third and final spring festival, also known as Shavuot. The firstfruits recognized during this festival are seven grains,[160] not just barley like in FFBH.

During Shavuot, seven grains are brought to the altar as a sacrifice. People everywhere bring their particular gift to the temple as thanks to G and a blessing to one another. Well, coincidentally enough, there are seven gifts of the Spirit,[161] and they vary by the individual. All people are expected to bring their gifts forward as thanks to G and a blessing to others. When all the gifts are brought together, there will be a fruitful harvest to offer and a wonderful celebration. Shauvot is not only the festival of the grains, it is a betrothal to the Almighty and a time to receive the Word of G.

Allow me to clarify. Two major events occurred on Pentecost, or Shavuot. First, this festival celebrates the day G came down to Mount Sinai and made covenant with the Israelites. Second, Pentecost is the

---

[160] The number seven has significance in Scripture. It represents perfection. The Hebrew seven is *shevah* (*shebah*), which comes from the root word *shava*, which means "to be full." Generally, when you see that number, you see completeness. G rested on the seventh day; the tabernacle was dedicated on the seventh day (after six days of construction); it took seven years for Solomon to build the temple; there are seven holy feasts; there are seven gifts of the Spirit and seven branches on a menorah; and the book of Revelation has seven churches, kings, hills, golden bowls, plagues, crowns, heads, thunders, trumpets, angels, eyes, horns, letters, stars, and many, many more.

[161] Check out Romans 12 for details on the gifts. You can also check out twelve Romans, but I don't think they will like it very much.

day Jesus sent the Holy Spirit to his people at the temple mount.[162] Two times G meets the faithful on a mountain, same bat time, same bat channel[163].

In the first covenant, the Word of G was written in stone,[164] because the people had specifically asked that G not speak to them directly. The second covenant marks the Word of G being written directly on the hearts of the people.

In the first covenant, in speaking with Moses, G made a deal with the people. G said, "Now if you obey me fully and keep my covenant, then out of all nations you will be my treasured possession. Although the whole earth is mine, you will be for me a kingdom of priests and a holy nation. These are the words you are to speak to the Israelites." So Moses conveyed this message to the people, and they accepted, all responding in one voice, "We will do everything the Lord has said."[165] There was an offer, an acceptance, and consideration. Contract formation has occurred.

According to Jewish custom, a marriage proposal was serious business, complete with an official contract between the families. There would not be a wild trip to Vegas with an electronic Elvis presiding. Instead, a solemn oath was given, and both sides agreed. The bride went away to wash and prepare herself for marriage. The groom's friend would present the bride during the ceremony. The

---

[162] Many people think that the Holy Spirit descended on the people in the upper room. While the disciples were in the upper room in Acts 1, in Acts 2—they were at the Temple mount. There are five points that support this: 1) the word for "house" in Acts 2 is also used for "Temple," 2) It was Pentecost—by tradition and command they were supposed to be at the Temple; 3) Scripture states they preached to thousands, each in their own tongue, which is hard to do in a house, much less the upper room of a house; 4) scripture states that thousands were immersed that day. That is really tough to do in one house even with robust plumbing. The only place in the city large enough to immerse thousands would be the Temple baths; and 5) G is known for revealing on mountains—Sinai in old covenant, Sinai for the commandments, the Mount of Transfiguration, Moriah for Abraham, etc.

[163] For those with a quirky sense of trivia.

[164] Namely, the Ten Commandments.

[165] Check out Exodus 19 for the original contract. Like a contract, it is usually written in fine print.

groom built a domed structure or canopy called a chuppah[166] and covered it with one of his garments, resembling a prayer shawl. Afterwards, the husband went to prepare a house, then brought the bride to their new location.

The first time G proposed to the people, G said, "I will take you as my own people, and I will be your G. Then you will know that I am the LORD your G, who brought you out from under the yoke of the Egyptians." The people shyly giggled, accepted the proposal, and then began making honeymoon plans. G truly and deeply desires an intimate relationship with the people. Just listen to G's words: "Later I passed by, and when I looked at you and saw that you were old enough for love, I spread the corner of my garment over you and covered your naked body. I gave you my solemn oath and entered into a covenant with you, declares the Sovereign Lord, and you became mine."[167]

When Moses shared the people's response, G instructed Moses and the Israelites to wash themselves and be sanctified for G's appearance;[168] much like a bride would do in preparation for a wedding. Moses traveled with the Israelites to Mount Sinai, which would act as the synagogue/church/altar/holy place for the wedding. The mountain shook, the earth rumbled. The people stood underneath the mountain.[169] The mountain itself was the chuppah. The Israelites panicked. Call it wedding-day jitters, nerves, or the sudden realization that they were committing themselves to the Creator, but they asked not to hear G's voice directly. It's shocking that anyone would not want to hear the ever-loving voice of G,[170] but to be fair, the Israelites were not used to the interactive pyrotechnics and earth-

---

[166] It is a fun word to say, especially if you do it with a Greek accent and throw one arm up in the air and toss your head back while pronouncing. It is an interactive word.

[167] Feel free to peruse Ezekiel for more information.

[168] A truly important act, given how much time they were hanging out in the desert. Seriously, have you ever smelled a camel? Bathing is crucial.

[169] The word in Scripture is "nether" which means underneath. That's some pretty impressive wedding preparation.

[170] The voice is better than Gabriel's.

moving effects.[171] They decided it was a bit overwhelming to hear directly from G. Hearing directly from G also heightens the level of personal accountability. So the people went to Moses and requested a slight amendment to the contract. The Israelites requested G speak only to Moses. Now, for a short-term plan, this seems like a good idea. You don't have as much pressure by having the actual Word of G before you. If you were seeking to sneak a bit of sin into your day, it would be a bit easier without the omniscient G talking to you.[172]

G honored the Israelites' change to the covenant and did not speak directly to them but agreed to communicate through Moses and other faithful men who became the mediators. The problem with this line of thinking is that with middle management comes bureaucracy. Instead of having an individual relationship with G, the Israelites had a list of rules—rules interpreted by the middle managers. That meant fallible men would continue creating their own rules and interpretations of the commands of G.

G respected the people's desire for an alternative to a personal relationship, even though G knew the alternative would lead to legalism, teachers of the law, and—gulp, dare I say it—lawyers. Although in those days the religious lawyers fell into camps, like Pharisees and Sadducees. While G's rules were all about how to love, the man-made rules became all about how to keep rules. The rules grew and grew and grew far bushier than G originally requested. But I digress….

Now the people had the mediator Moses. G pointed out something that their shortsightedness was missing—Moses wasn't going to be there forever. G agreed to accommodate the request, and, because this mediator would be temporary, further stated that G would send a "prophet likened unto Moses" and whoever does not listen to him will be held accountable.

So when does the new contract formation occur with prophet-likened-unto-Moses? Second verse, same as the first: on Pentecost,

---

[171] They did not have the opportunity to be desensitized by the high-tech special effects featured in the movies that later generations would witness.

[172] It's like attending a party with your parents is uncomfortable if you intend to do something naughty.

after the resurrection of the Messiah. The shift occurred from the perpetual need for a go-between to a direct relationship with G. Jesus, as promised, sent the Comforter, the Holy Spirit, on Pentecost. Now no longer would man need to teach man because they could all know G. Whether you admit it or not, there is that still, small voice within you that provides amazing comfort, guidance, and strength. Everyone has it but not everyone listens to it.

When the disciples were on the temple mountain celebrating Pentecost/Shavuot, the Spirit of G came down upon them, and the covenant was fulfilled in the original, desired form. Jeremiah foresaw this when he wrote, "'This is the covenant I will make with the people of Israel after that time,' declares the LORD. 'I will put my law in their minds and write it on their hearts. I will be their G, and they will be my people.'" The apostles did not receive additional commandments, or stone tablets. Instead, they were filled with the Holy Spirit, the eternal mediator who would help the people keep a personal relationship with G.

In the first covenant, G wrote on tablets of stone. In the second, G wrote on your hearts. The first covenant was written by the finger of G; the second, by G's spirit. In the first covenant, 3,000 people were slain; in the second, 3,000 live. The first covenant was the letter of the Torah; the second was the spirit of the Torah. The first covenant was on Mt. Sinai; the second was on Mt. Zion.[173]

It is not a coincidence that every major milestone of Jesus' life occurred on a massive holiday. It is prophetic. Think about it. For centuries before the birth of Christ, the Jewish people commemorated Passover, with its main focus of the rite being the death of a sacrificial lamb. Three days later they celebrated a happy festival. Fifty days later, yet another celebration commemorating the covenant with G. Jesus dies on Passover, and three days later he rises from the grave. Fifty days later he sends the Comforter[174] under a new covenant

---

[173] 1st Covenant info see: Exodus 24:12; 31:18;32:1–8; 32:26–28; 19:11 and the Torah, 2nd Covenant info can be found at: Jeremiah 31:33, Psalm 40:8; 37:31; Isaiah 51:7; Ezekiel 11:19, 20; 36:22–27; 2 Corinthians 3:3; 3:6; Hebrews 8:10;12:22; Acts 2:38–41; Romans 2:29; 7:6; 11:26 and 1 Peter 2:6

[174] The Holy Spirit, specifically, not a big down blanket.

to the people. The timing reconciles as well as the symbolism. The question, the answer; the prophecy, the fulfillment—the events tie together and cannot successfully be viewed in isolation. If you don't know prophecy, how do you know that Jesus fulfilled them?

On the flip side, if you have been practicing rituals for years, have you ever wondered, *What is the point of the rituals?* G doesn't do superfluous. G has a point to the requests that G makes. At some time, you would have to stop and ask, *Why did G request these specific actions at these specific times?*—especially in light of Old and Not-So-Old Testament Scriptures that proclaim the festivals are shadows of "things to come."

There are people who claim that Jesus never expressly mentioned he was the Messiah. These are the people who are only reading half of Scripture. You have to know the requirements for the position of Messiah before you can affirmatively state if they are or are not being fulfilled.

Think about when Jesus gave the Sermon on the Mount. Imagine you are sitting there, eating your lunch, listening to this itinerant preacher/rabbi going on about blessings. Keep in mind to whom Jesus was speaking. He wasn't speaking to pagans or people unfamiliar with Scripture, which in those days would have been only the Old Testament. His audience knew Scripture. They knew it well.

Anyway, Jesus begins, "Blessed are the poor in spirit." What would you think when you heard that? Why would you care? Would you respond, "Aw, how sweet. Blessing poor-spirit people. What a great guy." Um, maybe, but probably not. If all he wanted to do was to bless, Jesus could just have said, "Bless everyone. The end. Amen." Anyone could have sat down and randomly blessed various classes of people. These blessings were quite distinct, quite profound, and highly prophetic.

If you were a first-century Judean and you heard "Blessed are the poor in spirit," your mind would go to the most relevant scripture on that point. You would probably think back to the book of Isaiah, when Isaiah mentions that when the Messiah arrives, he will bless the poor in spirit.

What about "Blessed are those who mourn"? Again, the scripture to which Jesus speaks is found in Jeremiah[175] 31 and Isaiah 61, where teaching explained some things that would happen when the Messiah arrived.

Each blessing is tied to Old Testament prophecies. To the audience well versed in Scripture, the blessings came across as much more than niceties—they are bold proclamations.

How about when Jesus says, "Blessed are you when people persecute you for my name's sake"? If you knew Scripture, you would have already deduced from the previous blessings precisely who Jesus was claiming to be. If you didn't know Scripture, you would have to pause and say, "Wait a minute. Who are you?"

Seriously, what preacher ever said, "Wow, you are so lucky if people get mad at you because of me"? The first question you would have to ask is, "Who are you?" No one asked Jesus, because they had a clear understanding of Scripture, and he was very clear in his delivery.

He had to be careful how he positioned his comments so as not to violate the laws of the man. For instance, the term *son of man* meant two things in the first century. It meant your average Joe, or it meant the Messiah. When Jesus said he was the Son of Man, the religious leaders couldn't punish him. It was risky, it was dangerous, and it was pretty funny. Jesus lived on the edge.

ROSH HASHANAH—START OF JUDGMENT DAY

Rosh Hashanah has not yet been fulfilled, but it prophesies the catching away of the righteous and the start of the end of days. Rosh Hashanah is Hebrew for "head of the year." Think of it as a Hebrew New Year. It represents the start of the Jewish civil calendar. It is the anniversary of the day of creation, which falls on the first day of the month of Tishrei.[176] Since Jewish months are based on a lunar cycle, you can't equate that with an exact date on the Gregorian calendar—as

---

[175] He was a good friend of mine. I never understood a single word he said but....

[176] Interestingly enough, you can transpose the Hebrew letters "on the first of Tishri" and create the words "in the beginning." Pretty cool, eh?

the Gregorians never cared for much for what the moon was doing, but generally it falls in early fall. Rosh Hashanah prophesies the start of the end of days.

Interestingly enough, in the upcoming old days, Rosh Hashanah could take up to two days to celebrate, so it is sometimes called one long day. The reason for the two days is that the Jewish people had to wait until the first sighting of a new moon[177] officially to celebrate. Well, that was difficult to do when you had to start celebrating at sunset. Oftentimes the Jewish people would start celebrating on the day they believed to be Rosh Hashanah; if the new moon didn't appear that night (or the old moon did appear)—sweet, one more night to celebrate. So, no one really knew the hour or the day that the holiday would formally start, but they prepared just in case. Jesus made comments similar to this, as well. He said that no one would know the hour or day; of course, Jesus was referring to the ultimate Rosh Hashanah, but the sentiment was well established. Science will eventually afford people the ability to tell when the new moon will officially be in play, but even science can't predict the start of the end of days. The take-away is that since you do not know the precise time, you should live your life awake, alert and prepared.

Rosh Hashanah is also known in the Jewish community by a few other names, each with distinct symbolism. It is also called the Feast of Trumpets, or *Yom Teru'ah* ("day of the shofar blast"). A shofar is not a southern reference to distance; it is a ram's (or similar animal) horn used as a sort of trumpet.[178] One of the main blasts made by the horn is a blast called a *teruah*. There are two other blasts that can be done, but interesting enough the teruah was called out in the festival-naming convention. The teruah is a series of short blasts used as an alarm. When it wasn't Rosh Hashanah, the teruah was an alarm sounded to warn or to awake the people. When it is Rosh Hashanah, the sounding of the shofar on this special day serves an equivalent purpose. It is sounded to wake people from spiritual slumber so they can reconnect to the divine.

---

[177] Or the non-sighting of an old moon.

[178] Forged brass instruments and John Philip Sousa were unheard of at the time; thus, ram's horns were used. Later in time, silver horns were also used.

The Talmud states that on Rosh Hashanah the dead will be raised. This corresponds with Paul's comments about the dead rising at the last trump.[179] Paul's account of the end times reconciles with the beliefs surrounding this festival. Paul states "We shall not sleep, but we shall all be changed, in a moment, in the twinkling of an eye, at the last trumpet (shofar): for the trumpet (shofar) shall sound, and the dead shall be raised incorruptible, and we shall be changed." The Book of Revelation will also reference the blowing of the trumpet as a sort of starter pistol for the start of the end of days. Old and New Testaments reconcile Rosh Hashanah with the event of the last days; however, if you don't know the festivals, you will totally miss the prophetic connections in both Testaments.

Another nickname of Rosh Hashanah is Day of the King. Ancient writings reveal that on Rosh Hashanah, the people were to recite verses relating to sovereignty, remembrance, and shofar blasts. The sovereignty was so that people would proclaim G as king; prophetically, it is the coronation of the Messiah. G is the King of all the earth. G's coronation occurred at Creation, Tishri 1, the first Rosh Hashanah. This day is a reminder and a tribute to that fact. The kings of Israel were to be coronated on Rosh Hashanah, and this is the day that Messiah also will be coronated.

Interestingly enough, one of the psalms recited on Rosh Hashanah about the sovereignty of the Lord (Psalm 45) also correlates with a bride being prepared to meet her groom. Many times throughout Scripture, the faithful[180] are referred to as the bride of the Messiah.[181] This scripture speaks of the bride being led to her king.

Rosh Hashanah is aptly known as the Day of Judgment. Since many Christians fail to explore the Jewish heritage, they totally miss the prophecy surrounding this sacred day. G was very clear with this one. It is called the Day of Judgment. Christians often wax philosophical about what might and may occur on "judgment day," but the foreshadowing and the outline have quite clearly been provided. There are Christians who argue, "How can the Day of Judgment be

---

[179] Not a card game, a horn.

[180] Also known as those written in the Book of Life.

[181] This works on many levels, especially since the people are betrothed on Shavout!

affiliated with judgment day?" To that, all I can say is ... well, there isn't really anything I can say.

The Talmud states that three books are opened on Rosh Hashanah: the Book of the Righteous, the Book of the Wicked, and the Book of the Undecided. The first two are pretty easy. The Book of the Righteous contains the names of the people who are just that—righteous. The Book of the Wicked contains the names of, well, the wicked. The Book of the Undecided contains the names of those people who have yet to truly make up their minds by the way they live and the choices they make. On Rosh Hashanah, G consolidates the three books to two: the Book of the Righteous and the Book of the Wicked. The Book of Revelation states that "anyone's name not found in the Book of Life will be thrown into the lake of fire."

There is a ten-day grace period between Rosh Hashanah and Yom Kippur that is called the Days of Awe. By your repentance, prayer, and good deeds in the time between Rosh Hashanah and Yom Kippur, you can plea to have G's decree altered. There are three ways to prepare for Rosh Hashanah. Turn to G, turn to those whom you have harmed and turn to those in need. This is the time for thoughtful reflection, atonement, and prayer. Where would you like to spend eternity? If you don't choose, G will choose for you. G inscribes each person's fate into a book and waits until Yom Kippur to seal the verdict.

For those people who believe the Old Testament was replaced or otherwise done away with, it is important to note that if you don't know the tradition of Rosh Hashanah or Yom Kippur, then you won't get most of the Book of Revelation or various other references in books such as Hebrews. Absent the Old Testament, reading much of the New Testament would be like drinking excessive amounts of alcohol before reading a Lewis Carroll book, with all sorts of strange creatures, except for the White Rabbit,[182] popping in and out of the story line. I have seen many a Christian decide to start studying Scripture by first perusing a book like Revelation. Studying the Bible without knowing the Old Testament and the Gospels is a lot like building a bookcase by reading only the last two steps in

---

[182] There are goats and dragons and beasts ... Oh! My!

the process in Chinese and never having looked at what the final product should be.[183]

YOM KIPPUR—SENTENCING

Rosh Hashanah kicks off the "Days of Awe" and leads to Yom Kippur. As I said earlier, the Days of Awe are days between the two festivals and are a time of introspection for an individual to consider and repent from their sins. This festival has five separate services to attend. Why so many? This day is your final appeal. This is the last chance to plead for inclusion into the Book of Life. Yom Kippur is the day the names are sealed into their respective books. Yom Kippur has some very prophetic traditions. Much like Passover, which left people pondering what G has against lambs, Yom Kippur might trigger the question, *What does G have against left-handed goats?* Boy, I bet that question got you wondering too.

Perhaps I should begin with giving you some insight about the rituals surrounding Yom Kippur. On this day a ceremony was performed to purge the defilement from the Temple and the people. This ceremony required that a bull and two goats be sacrificed.[184]

A bull gets sacrificed first as atonement for the sins of the priests and their households. Keep in mind that Jesus is the atonement for humans; therefore, he is represented by the bull. He goes in the house of G first to atone for sins. The priest must carry the blood of the bull into the Holy of Holies and sprinkle it on the cover of the Ark of the Covenant. No one can touch the priest until this has occurred; much like when Jesus first appeared to Mary and told her not to lay hands on him because he had not yet gone to G.

Consider this in context of the Book of Hebrews which states "But when Christ came as high priest of the good things that are now already here, as he went through the greater and more perfect tabernacle that is

---

[183] The good thing about reading Revelation early is that you find out early that the good guys win.

[184] The ceremonies described here can be found in the Talmud (a central text serving as the basis for all code of Rabbinic Law). Talmud contains the Mishnah and the Gemara. The Mishnah is the written Oral Torah (sounds like an oxymoron but it's not) and the Gemara is the explanation of the Mishnah.

not made by human hands … He did not enter by means of the blood of goats and calves; but entered the Most Holy Place once for all by his own blood, thus obtaining eternal redemption." Fascinating, isn't it?

Next, there was a lottery involving goats.[185] Two goats were brought to the eastern gate of the temple. The high priest[186] drew lots over two goats. One goat was selected "for the Lord" and one "for Azazel." Miraculously enough, the goat for the Lord almost always was on the right-hand side; the other lot fell to the goat on the left "for Azazel." The high priest tied a red band around the horns of the goat "for Azazel." Another scarlet band was tied at the Temple.

I should pause for a moment here. Most Christian texts do not translate the Hebrew words "for Azazel" true to form. In many translations, the word *scapegoat* is used. That is a bit of a misnomer. The second goat was never intended to represent some unfortunate schmuck who was innocent but forced to suffer for someone else's misdoings. This translation makes it look like the goat represents the gullible. Not the case. Azazel is a demon who is credited for doing many naughty, horrible, and evil things. He gets credit for teaching men to fashion weapons for war, for teaching women how to adorn themselves with jewelry and makeup for the art of seduction, and for teaching witchcraft—as some of his more popular skills. The left-handed goat does not represent the suckers of the world (well, not in a superficial sense). The goat for Azazel represents the fate of those who follow the lawless or evil one.

The right goat for the Lord represents the fate of the righteous. Keep in mind that life is in the blood. What becomes of the blood is synonymous with what becomes of the life. The high priest laid his hands on the goat for the Lord and pronounced confession on behalf of the priests. He then slaughtered the goat and received its blood in a bowl. The high priest took the goat's blood into the Holy of Holies. The goat's blood could not be put on the altar unless and until it has joined with the blood of the atonement (the bull's blood). Ultimately, this message is that the lives of those "for the Lord" must be joined with the eternal sacrifice, Jesus, to enter the house of G.

---

[185] This one did not involve six winning numbers.

[186] High in esteem and rank, not altitude.

Now, about that goat on the left. The high priest would lean his hands on the goat for Azazel and confess the sins of the entire people of Israel; the people would still confess privately just to keep the conversation going. The goat for Azazel would be chased off into the wilderness. This goat was led to a cliff outside Jerusalem and pushed off its edge where its carcass became food for the beasts of field and birds of the air. Interestingly enough, there was a miracle associated with this act. Once the goat fell, the scarlet cords on its horn and the temple would be made white as snow. The people rightfully understood this to mean their sins were forgiven. Interestingly enough, this miracle ceased around the year of 30 AD/CE—roughly the time of Jesus' death. The final sacrifice was made.

The Book of Hebrews and Leviticus agree that blood must be shed for the remission of sins. The Talmud also agrees that "There is no atonement without blood." You may think that it is rather barbaric to have all this killing to make up transgressions. But sacrifices were established for several reasons.

First, G *limited* what animals could be killed. Remember, there were groups and tribes of people throughout history that would sacrifice other people, virgins, or children. This was so appalling to G, that setting clear sacrifice boundaries prevented the Jewish people from crossing such horrid lines.

Second, G demanded that the animals could not suffer. There simply must be humanity in the sacrifice. Unfortunately, such compassion was not extended to G's son.

Third, a person's flocks were their assets. It would cost people to sin. Beyond the pseudo-financial impact, it should cause a person significant pause when they look an innocent animal in the eye and know that his personal sin is why that animal is to die. Knowing the financial and conscious consequence of sin should act as a significant deterrent in committing sins.

Fourth, the sacrifices *foreshadow* the Messiah.[187] The rituals surrounding Yom Kippur are highly prophetic of the sacrifice of

---

[187] The Book of Hebrews offers a lot of insight on the correlation between Yom Kippur and Jesus' sacrifice. FYI: Hebrews is a New Testament book, not a mandate that men make coffee—**HE**-brews.

Jesus. It provides insight into how the Messiah opened the door for the righteous to enter eternal bliss. It also shows the fate of those who turn their backs on G. Like the goat for the Lord, the righteous will join with the sin offering and go into the house of G. Like the goat for Azazel, the wicked will be cast into an abyss where they will become carnage, basically.

One amazing reference to this is found in Matthew 25:31–46. Jesus flatly states that when the Son of Man comes, the sheep will be on his right and goats on his left.[188] The sheep on the right will share in the kingdom of G and have eternal life, but the goats on the left will suffer eternal punishment. This isn't to say that G wants people to suffer; far be it. Much like Adam and Eve, G affords you free will. Separation from G is, in and of itself, hell.

SUKKOT—MESSIAH'S BIRTHDAY

The festival of Sukkot prophesies the birth of Messiah and the joyous celebration afforded those born into the Messiah's kingdom. Before I get too much into the birth of the star of the show[189] and the correlation with the festival of Sukkot, I should mention the opening act—the birth of John the Baptist. I need to address him first as Scripture foretold that Elijah would precede the Messiah. John is the Elijah who was to come, and addressing his birth is important in elaborating on the timing and prophecy of the birth of Jesus.

Check out the beginning of Luke. John the Baptist's father, Zechariah, was a priest in the division of Abijah. The book of Chronicles will elaborate on how the priests were to serve by their divisions twice a year. Since the shifts rotated, each division's service would fall in the beginning and latter part of the year with roughly six months between. The first division would serve in the first week, then the second in the second, then the third in the third, and so on and so on until all the divisions served, and then the cycle would resume. All the priests worked during the festivals where a pilgrimage had to

---

[188] The reason "sheep" and "goats" were used here in the right/left separation is that sheep follow the voice of their shepherd. Goats follow their own will.

[189] Pun intended.

occur; this includes Sukkot—and Passover and Pentecost. This means the average priest worked five weeks a year, as festivals don't count in the rotation cycles.

Now, going back to the book of Chronicles, you will learn that Abijah (Zechariah's division) served during the eighth shift. Counting off eight weeks from the first of Nisan, Zechariah had his scheduled work time falling the week before Pentecost. Now jump to the book of Luke, to Zechariah's time in the temple. His division was on duty, and Zechariah was chosen to go into the temple and burn incense while the other priests hung out outside and prayed. It's important to note that the selection to go into the temple for this event was made by lot and was a once-in-a-lifetime event. Once the priest was selected, his name was removed from the pool of lots,[190] and he wouldn't get the opportunity again.

When the priests prayed before the altar of incense, they prayed a prayer called the Amidah, or the Standing Prayer.[191] The priests didn't chat randomly with G by making personal requests or general confession during this event. Zechariah is praying the standard and mandated request to *bring forth a redeemer*. Then an angel appears, with a smooth, silky voice, and scares the boogers out of Zechariah.[192] The angel, after going through the standard protocol referenced in the footnote, proceeds to tell Zechariah that his prayer will be answered. A lot of people get mixed up on this point. They think that Zechariah was praying for a kid. I'll give you that Zechariah was without a child, but that wasn't the prayer Zechariah was making. If that was what he was asking for, he would have been remiss in his priestly duties, and that would not have caused G to show such great favor. No, G was answering the request for a redeemer.

---

[190] Unlike Abraham's early vacation spot—Lot's pool. Ha-ha.

[191] It goes something like this: "Blessed are you, Lord our G. G of our fathers … who brings a Redeemer."

[192] This is the most common response to seeing an angel, which is why the standard operating procedure for an angel requires that the first line said in the face of a petrified listener is "Do not be afraid."

To start the preparation for the Messiah, the angel gave some rather explicit directions on child raising.[193] The angel stated that John (the baby to be) would be bestowed with the Holy Spirit and possess the power of Elijah. This last statement is pretty powerful, as the Jewish people for centuries have awaited the return of Elijah. They rightfully believe Elijah will usher forth the Messiah. In fact, they have—and still do—set an extra plate at the Seder table for none other than Elijah, because he was expected to come at Passover.

Now, by the time Zechariah gets back to his wife and gets to multiplying in order to ensure that the angel's directives come true, you will have John's due date somewhere around early to mid Nisan. And what holiday falls at this time? Passover! So John was born and welcomed at Passover, just a prophesied and expected. Jesus will go so far as to flat-out state in the book of Matthew that John is the "Elijah who was to come."

Stay in the Gospels, but flip to the book of John. This book will let you know that there were six months between John's and Jesus' birth. That brings Jesus' birth to the *festival of Sukkot*.

The ceremonial requirements for the Feast of Sukkot, also called the Feast of Tabernacles, can be found in the book of Numbers,[194] and in the Book of Leviticus. This festival is the most joyous celebration and is of utmost importance![195] It was so important that all Jewish men, women, and children *had* to make a pilgrimage to Jerusalem every seven[196] years for the festival.

So every seven years, the pilgrimage to Jerusalem for the festival was mandatory for *all* men, women, and children—even a woman nine months pregnant—to attend. In those days, a man could travel alone to register his family for a census, which took place over a

---

[193] General temperament, name, drinking prohibitions—you know, the general parenting advice that you don't find in routine baby-raising literature.

[194] There are also letters in this book. A book of just numbers wouldn't have been very fulfilling.

[195] This festival was such a joyous event that it was said in ancient writings that "he who has not witnessed the rejoicing at the water-drawing huts has, throughout the whole of his life, witnessed no real rejoicing."

[196] Remember, the number seven has divine import.

period of months and was conveniently located just a few miles away from the festivities, but he couldn't leave the family behind on the seventh year Sukkot. Joseph didn't have to take Mary with him for a census; he had to take her for Sukkot. Since *all* Jews were required to go to Jerusalem for the pilgrimage, it would not be uncommon for travelers to overflow out of Jerusalem and stay a few miles outside of town, say in a place like Bethlehem.[197]

Sukkot is the plural of *sukkah*, which means a booth, tent, hut, or temporary dwelling. The word for *sukkah* is the same root word that can also reference an animal lair. Scripture requires practicing Jews to stay outside in a tent or booth, so custom dictates that the Jewish people spend the nights—or at least a minimal a portion of their days—in a hut-like structure, very much like what you would see in nativity sets at Christmastime. Joseph and Mary were staying in a sukkah for the birth of Jesus, as were many other Jewish people because the festival warranted it. It is a good thing that Jesus was born in a temporary dwelling. Had he been born in a hotel, celebrations as humans will come to know them would be markedly different and more commercialized than ever.

The basis for staying in the booths is a historical commemoration of the protection of the Jewish people in the wilderness after the exodus from Egypt. In essence, this time allows the Jewish people to go into their own wilderness in order to reflect on G's grace and give thanks. In the wilderness, the Jewish people left their homes and stayed in a temporary dwelling; just as Jesus left his heavenly home to stay in the earthly temporary dwelling.[198] It is in a *sukkah* that the woman, Mary, sat in a reflective wilderness and gave birth to a son. In this wilderness she was protected from those who would seek to harm her and her baby.

If you go to the Gospel of Matthew, you will learn how magi from the east went to visit the baby Jesus. While many Christians sing about the kings who came to visit the Messiah, the proper translation of *magi* would equate more to "rav" or "rabbi." These are highly

---

[197] Bethlehem is about five miles from Jerusalem. Scripture expressly stated that the Messiah would be born in Bethlehem.

[198] John 1:14

esteemed men, learned in the studies of Jewish Scripture, who paid a visit to the baby. This also makes a bit more sense since it was the religious leaders who watched the stars to know the seasons and times of sacred events.[199]

Studying the stars outside of a scriptural basis equates to astrology, and this is a no-no with G. The difference between astronomy and astrology is likened to sodium chloride and sodium *and* chloride. The former spices things up. The latter will kill you; you'd better know the difference if you decide to start playing with it. The moon and stars do tell of events to come, but they were not placed to benefit any one human's personal goal. The signs are to tell of holy events, not personal luck or ambition. It is a great foothold for old Lucifer when humans start dabbling in astrology. This is why G warns against such behavior.

Sorry, back to the story. The magi came from the east, Babylon actually. While Babylon is noted as the upcoming-and-coming Sodom or Gomorrah, there were devout men in the city. Back in the day of Daniel, many Jewish men were captured and taken to Babylon as prisoners. Despite all the sin and corruption around them, there were those who were able to maintain a holy life. Daniel himself is evidence of this fact. Well, the Jewish people knew the Messiah would be born in Bethlehem; Scripture was clear on this point. A Jewish Midrash written hundreds of years before Jesus' birth proclaimed that in the week the Messiah would be born there would be a bright star in the east. Holy men studied the stars to learn this date.

At the end of the first day of Sukkot, the priests would light four huge lamps in the temple court, each with four huge bowls. Interestingly enough, the wicks for the lamps were made from swaddling clothes, the worn-out undergarments of the priests; funny how the swaddling clothes served as a mechanism for bringing light into the world. When the lamps were all lit, they illuminated the entire city of Jerusalem so much so that the Temple was called "The Light of the World."[200] The dancing and singing would crescendo into a great

---

[199] Per G's comment during creation's fourth day.

[200] Shortly after the last day of the festival, Jesus will proclaim "I am the Light of the World."

celebration. This rejoicing lasted throughout the night. Not only does this day rightly celebrate the birth of the Messiah, it mirrors what each human will experience when born into the Kingdom of G.

Part of the ritual of Sukkot involved sacrificing a set of animals each day. Now, to most people this may sound pretty harsh, but there are many things to be kept in mind. The early people killed their own animals to eat, to make clothes, to make weapons, and to make tools; they didn't buy them pre-killed or off the rack. Killing animals wasn't done frivolously. It was done for survival.

Sukkot is also a blessing for all the nations. It was that time of year when the priests prayed for all the other nations of the world. I mentioned animal sacrifices a bit earlier. Well, on the first day of the celebration, thirteen bulls were killed; the next day, twelve; then eleven and so on, until the seventh day. If you count up the number of bulls, you will find that there were seventy in all. Seventy has a pretty interesting meaning.[201] It is the combination of two perfect numbers—seven and ten; it is perfection with a purpose. It suggests spiritual order, purpose, and significance. Why would there be seventy bulls? Because there are seventy nations[202] and this is a time to pray for others. Each bull was an atonement sacrifice for another nation. The Israelites prayed for every nation and peace to all nations, not just their own. Seventy bulls, seventy nations, and lots of prayers and celebrating mark the first week of the festival.

Scripture was clear that the Messiah was not just for the Jewish people; this affirmation is found in both the Old and the Not-So-Old Testaments. In the later chapters of Genesis, through the promise to Abraham, "all nations" would be blessed. The prophet Haggai wrote that G "will shake all nations, and the desire of all nations will come." That Old Testament talk was revalidated by Paul in his letter to the Ephesians, and it is also found in Revelation. All nations were to be blessed by the Messiah.

---

[201] Seventy Israelites went into Egypt, seventy priests comprise the Sanhedrin (the supreme court of Jews), and Jesus chose seventy disciples.

[202] In Deuteronomy 32, the Most High gives inheritances and set up boundaries in accordance with the sons of Israel. There were seventy. These nations are mentioned in the story of the tower of Babel. For divine purposes there are seventy nations.

G would not and does not select a person based on birthright or religious identification but on rebirth and identification with G. In fact, G demonstrated this several times throughout history. Whereas tradition and custom mandated certain people be empowered with rights and riches by virtue of their birth order, G turned it upside down and elected another to receive the gifts.

For instance, Isaac was not Abraham's firstborn, but he was selected to bring forth G's promise to Abraham. Jacob was not the firstborn. David was not firstborn. Moses was not the firstborn. This isn't to say being first was without value, as there were firstborns who were selected by G.[203] The point is that human custom and tradition devised outside of the will of G mean little to G. G picks elect people based solely on what is on the inside.

On each day after the first day of the festival, a gaggle of priests would set out to gather some seriously large willow branches to wave back and forth in a procession on the way to the temple. The willows were so large they would make a swooshing sound, much like the sound of the wind commonly associated with the *ruach*—or Holy Spirit.

While the willow wavers were walking, another group of priests would proceed to the pool of Siloam from which the priest would fill a vessel with water. The Talmud would state that the Spirit of Happiness was drawn here. Whoever witnessed the event would draw happiness for the soul and salvation from travail. Since the water was moving, flowing, and not stagnate, it was known as living water.

There are many interesting points about the pool from which water was drawn for the festival. *Siloam* translates to "sent one," the transliteration of the word is *apostle* or *missionary*. The Messiah was identified as the "sent one" on several occasions, and that is about as apostolic as one can possibly be. Siloam is fed from a source known as the Virgin Spring, or Virgin Fount (En-rogel), just as Messiah sprung from a virgin. It is not without import that Jesus sent the blind man to wash in this pool,[204] as Jewish writings clearly stated that this was the Messiah's pool.

---

[203] Like Jesus.

[204] See John for more detail. Well, read John for more detail.

The waving windy willow branches then went to the temple, with the water bearers leading the way. In essence, you could say the Living Water escorted in the Spirit.[205]

Once at the temple, the willows were placed around the altar, thereby creating a little *sukkah* —or hut. At one point, the priest would pour the water on the altar. Since the priest with the water was hiding in the new willow booth, the people in attendance could not see if the water had been poured out. So they would ask. A priest, standing between the pourer and the people, would raise his arm as the water was being poured, so all would know that the water of salvation was being poured out.

On the last day, instead of circling the altar one time, the priests circled it seven times and sang with loud voices a song of redemption and salvation—"Save now, I pray, O Lord; O Lord, I pray, send now prosperity. Blessed is he who comes in the name of the Lord."

> On the last day of the feast, the great day, Jesus stood and cried out, 'If anyone thirsts, let him come to me and drink. He who believes in me, as the Scripture has said, "Out of his heart will flow rivers of living water."

Jesus said those remarkable words during Sukkot, but most people miss the most critical part of the verse. While Jesus was correctly revealing his identity and how the prophetic actions correlate to his life, the most overlooked yet profound part of that verse are the words "*Jesus stood*." You see, the people are before the altar. You did not sit in this area of the temple. In fact, the only person who could sit in this area was a king descended from David. Most later-day Scripture readers read this verse and imagine a modern church service with everyone seated uncomfortably upright in hard wooden pews. That is not how things were done in the temple, especially in front of the altar. The fact that Jesus "stood" meant that he had to have been sitting, and sitting in this area would not and did not go unnoticed. The fact that he was sitting also explains the conversation

---

[205] There would also be a flute player in the procession. Interestingly enough, the word for flute also translates to "pierced one".

that ensued after he made this claim. The conversation immediately went to references of the Christ, the Messiah. The people were not making a leap in going there. Jesus spoke with authority, and his statement alone may have created some conversation, much like if someone blurted out commentary during a minister's homily. But his statement was taken more seriously, because he combined with it with a most dramatic and drastic action.

Oh yeah, I forgot to mention, Jesus made this statement on the last day of the feast called *Hoshana Rabbah*—"The Great Salvation."

There is one other amazing fact that I would be remiss in my duties to overlook. If you calculate from the birth of Christ at Sukkot to his conception date you would arrive at the festival of Chanukah. The back story to this festival is fascinating. It wasn't one of the ordained festivals in the Old Testament; in fact, you won't find reference to this holiday at all in the Old Testament. You will find it in extra-Biblical sources and, ironically enough, in the New Testament.

The Jewish people were being severely persecuted by a man named Antiochus Epiphanes[206] whose barbaric acts against the Jews can only be compared to that of Hitler's. In addition to the atrocities against the people, he stopped their worship services and practices. Antiochus had pigs sacrificed on the altar in the Temple. You can imagine the desecration this unclean animal created on the altar of G. The Jews revolted against the forces of assimilation and reclaimed their lives and the Temple.

They cleared and cleaned the Temple but need to rededicate it. There was only enough oil to burn the menorah, which was supposed to burn continuously, for one night. Miraculously, the oil burned for eight nights, the time it took to make more oil.

This festival represents the victory of faith and commitment to G. It is the miracle of light restoring the connection between the people and G. How appropriate that Jesus would be conceived on this day![207]

---

[206] "Epiphanes" means "God made manifest". The Jewish people referred to him as "Epimanes" or "the mad man."

[207] John 8:12

KINGDOM OF G

Oh, but I have been rambling about the messianic prophecies. I remember Adam looming there in the background. Just as Adam and Eve pulled the stunt that unleashed worry, panic, and ultimately sin into the world; Jesus ushered in the kingdom of G—an internal and external means of salvation from the bondage of sin.

Jesus brought forth the kingdom of G. But what exactly is the kingdom of G? It isn't a tangible thing. It is the power of G released through the individual. It is the power to love, to create, to heal, to comfort, and to live. What suppresses the kingdom of G is the introduction of sin, worry, and pride, which also aren't tangible things. They can have tangible effects but are not tangible.

When evil was granted authority, it didn't seize it by virtue of formal appointment, office, or position. A tangible king, president, czar, or ruler did not ascend to a throne. Most religions agree on this point. Here's where the confusion set in. Many people interpreted Scripture to mean that the Messiah would be a worldly king, offering physical vengeance and wielding worldly power.

This is where the disconnect occurs. The spiritual battles wage all around, but pain and evil spring from within. Humans don't choose bad because of a physical trait or tangible problem. The choice comes from each person's heart. A worldly king can force external behaviors, but only a spiritual king can call forth internal change. The Messiah did not come to manipulate the external battles, or else no one would be prompted to change from within.

In certain parts of the world, when people want to restrain an elephant, they tie a small rope to the elephant's leg. They stake the other end of the rope to the ground. When an elephant goes to move, it feels the restraint and ceases its attempt to walk. It believes it is trapped. The elephant is a prisoner. But the elephant is much stronger than its bondage. If it simply exerts a portion of its power, it can be free. This is what the Messiah is to humans. Scripture never suggested the Messiah would, metaphorically, run to all elephants, undo the ropes, and smite those who tied them up. He simply calls to those in bondage so that they may come to him and be free. The freedom from bondage and the ability to resist the bondage is what, by default, punishes the taskmasters. A taskmaster without a slave is impotent.

When Adam and Eve were thrown from the garden, they lost access to the eternal life granted by the Tree of Life, because their hearts yielded to the antithesis to life as evidenced by their words and actions. The Tree of Life did not disappear; it simply was guarded by that flaming sword.[208] The Messiah who wields that sword points out two important distinctions in Scripture.

First, Jesus distinguishes between the rules of G and the rules of man. G made some pretty specific statements in the Old(er) Testament. People added to those rules until it became a crazy, legalistic burden appreciated only by contract lawyers and used-car salesmen. When Jesus did things that appeared contrary to law, it was only *man's* law that was refuted. Jesus did not ever disregard G's laws. Jesus was very clear that he did not abolish the Torah or the law.[209] Jesus fulfilled it. Many Christians have totally come to disregard the Old Testament, as though it were superseded and replaced. But if you hold tightly to the New Testament, you simply must recognize the Old. The other primary reason for not excluding Old Testament study is the other point made by Jesus.

Second, the rules were not to be the penultimate peak or goal but the foundation, the *minimum* standard. Jesus didn't say ignore the rules, he said to strive to go above and beyond them. The Torah said not to commit adultery. Jesus said not even to look at another woman lustfully. Scripture said not to kill, but Jesus said even being angry with a brother or sister is equal to breaking this law. The rules were not the ceiling to which you should strive. They are the floor, the minimum expectations, and each human should strive to rise above the physical trappings. It makes sense too. No person would ever want to hear from a spouse that the spouse has never *actually* cheated on him or her but *has* fantasized about being with many other people. No one could truly love if, although he'd never actually killed someone, he had wished for others to die or experience tragedy. Jesus upped the ante from only actions to actions *and* thoughts.

---

[208] Oddly enough, Uriel had nothing to do with it.

[209] See Matthew 5:17.

By truly loving people, you should automatically be keeping the laws, as all of the laws hang on love. The rule is to love—but not love in any one person's subjective understanding of that word—because let's face it, some humans have a pretty warped sense of love. If your version of love deviates from Scripture, you may want to reconsider how you are loving or have loved people.

In the legal realm, there are two issues that underlie a crime, the *actus reus* and *mens rea*. The *actus reus* is the objective, external elements of *an action*, and the *mens rea* plays more into the *intent or motivation* behind that action. The Old Testament was interpreted by man to prescribe how you should *act*, the *actus reus*. In truth, it did offer insight on basic, simple actions to help people play well with others. But instead of contemplating why those rules were created, people begin to create more rules. Seeking G became an exercise of form over function. Jesus, in the New Testament, explains that you must also get control over your *thoughts*, the *mens rea*, to find happiness in this world and the next.

What Jesus resurrected[210] was that each human had the power to choose life or death.[211] Jesus taught that preventing the body from sinning and doing good were only half the battle; humans simply must control their thoughts. This was the missing link. It was never about going through the motions. It was all about disciplining the heart to love. Once a person masters his or her own thoughts, the heart follows. Once the heart becomes disciplined to love, the actions follow. This is why Jesus quoted Deuteronomy and stated that you should love "the Lord your G with all your heart and with all your soul and with *all your mind* and with all your strength."[212] The mind simply has to be controlled and focused on G.

---

[210] Besides Lazarus.

[211] Or as staunch Baptists would say, "Heaven or hell?" Or as staunch Baptist waitresses would say, "Nonsmoking or smoking section?"

[212] Some have proffered that these attributes are the roles of the Trinity. The heart: Jesus; the soul: the Holy Spirit; and the mind: G. The culmination of the three would be strength.

Jesus showed humans how to get back to the Tree of Life because he brought the Kingdom of G forth.[213] John the Baptist spoke of Jesus when he proclaimed that the kingdom of G was at hand. Jesus ushered in the kingdom by showing people that every human is wired for glory. G is the power plant, the source of the power, and all people can choose to flick the switch deep within their spirits.

Before Jesus arrived, uncleanliness was contagious. If you touched or ate something unclean—you were unclean. If you touched a sick person, a dead person, a bleeding person, a house where a dead person was—you were unclean. Extensive were the regulations about things that would render you unclean. Jesus changed all that. You can imagine how this baffled the religious leaders.

For example, if you touched a bleeding woman, you would be unclean. If you were bleeding, you certainly would *never* touch a holy man. Never, ever, ever. If you did, you would make that holy man unclean and therefore unable to perform his proper priestly duties.

There was a woman who was bleeding who touched Jesus. Instead of Jesus becoming unclean, the woman was made clean.

Leprosy would certainly make you unclean, but Jesus made the lepers clean.

If you touched a dead person, you were deemed unclean. When Jesus touched a dead person, he brought the person to life. In fact, Jesus had only to say the word, and the dead lived!

You can just imagine Jesus walking into the home where the little dead girl was lying. The priests were ready to pounce like tigers to proclaim Jesus unclean. Instead, the girl returned to life. What was the rule now? Was Jesus unclean? How could he be? Death fled.

What happens when you touch an unclean person whose source of uncleanliness disappears? See, now there is a new power working. Uncleanliness wasn't contagious, it was cured. The kingdom of G was unfolding before the eyes of those who were awaiting its return.

When Adam sinned, people had to ask the question, *If I can't trust him, whom can I trust? He seemed like such a nice boy.* Fear permeated. Sickness took hold. Judgment, anger, and violence erupted and spread like a cancer.

---

[213] Well, first ...

Now there stood a man undoing the harm that had been done. Now there was a man evidencing the glory of G. Now there was someone who could show people what they can have if they will only believe in the power of G. The healing power of G, the compassion of G, the love of G now are manifesting themselves in the actions of the Tree of Life.

Once the kingdom of G was introduced through Jesus, Jesus empowered others. The disciples could perform miracles. Other people could perform miracles in the name of G.

Jesus told his disciples to go out into the towns closest to Jerusalem and then slowly to spread outward. The kingdom of G was bursting forth like a spring out of Jerusalem.[214]

Jesus instructed the disciples to take nothing but what they had on. What they carried, wore, and how they performed mirrored what the priests wore when they entered the temple. The believers were now like priests walking into newly formed holy land, constantly increasing the size and scope of the holy area. It was no longer limited to the Holy of Holies, the temple, or even Jerusalem. The kingdom was at hand and afoot. The kingdom came.

It came right on time. The first-century Jewish priests believed there would be two thousand years of desolation, two thousand years of Torah, two thousand years of the Messiah, and then one thousand years of the kingdom of G. The desolation is the time without any Scripture. Think about it: Abraham didn't have a Bible, a Torah, or any other written text. He found G in a period of desolation solely by building a really great relationship with the power that he knew existed beyond just him. Two thousand years later, Moses received the Torah[215]. Roughly two thousand years after G gave the instructions brings the timing of the Messiah[216] right around the first

---

[214] Jerusalem is considered G's place, as G said "I will put my name there." The Jewish people write the name of G as "The name that should not be spoken." The first letter of the name is represented by the letter *shin*. If you look at a topographical map of Jerusalem, you will see that the topography of Jerusalem mirrors the holy letter symbolizing G's name.

[215] A.k.a the Word of G in written form.

[216] A.k.a. the Word of G manifest

century. By coming in the first century, Jesus satisfied scholarly belief about the overall timing of events. Next came two thousand years of the Messiah. To suggest the Messiah hasn't come would mean G got the dates wrong. G doesn't do wrong.

The book of Daniel also foretold successive empires—Babylonian, Medes/Persian, Greek, and Roman—and then a giant stone[217] would strike this last kingdom and would spread throughout the earth. Since Daniel made this prophecy before the Medes and Persians took power, you have to admit it was pretty remarkable—and accurate. Again, it means the Messiah needed to arrive during the Roman Empire or else G got the dates wrong, but we already talked about that.

Jesus arrived in the prophesied century, the prophesied day at the prophesied place by the prophesied parent through the prophesied lineage. And do you want to know what the Kingdom will be like after this life? Go back and read about the rejoicing at Sukkot. Your mind cannot fathom the joy, happiness and constant celebration that await the believer who enters the Kingdom.

GETTING TO THE TREE OF LIFE

There are two basic steps to reach the Tree of Life, but only one way. The two steps are *actions* and *thoughts*. I have told you a great deal about the beginning of Genesis to help lessen the pain that most humans encounter when reading Scripture. It shouldn't be as painful as many make it. There are some crazy and interesting nuances in the text that are completely overlooked. It is important to read, because Scripture, among other things, prescribes actions.

But actions are in vain if not accompanied by proper thought. What Scripture is to actions, prayer is to thoughts. I haven't been too detailed about prayer up until now, but I simply can't ignore it, and I don't want to undervalue it. Communication is essential in every relationship. You would never think to go to work, make dinner, and clean the house while never speaking to your spouse or children.

---

[217] Which should not be taken for granite.

That would be silly. To draw close to someone, you need to turn to them. Share.

Of course, actions and thoughts need to have guardrails. You don't just say and do whatever you want. I've heard many people say that they have prayed to G but their prayers weren't answered, but they don't really know for what they should be asking.

Scripture helps you understand what you should be asking for and seeking when you pray. Scripture reminds you to seek *first* G's kingdom and righteousness – *then* the gifts will be added. G will give you everything good, but you can't know good unless you know G. This is what prayer does, it allows you to take the gleanings from Scripture to learn of G and receive G's gifts. G won't give you everything. G is not Santa Claus. Getting everything is not the answer. If your child asked you to provide everything he or she would ever need, you may quickly agree to the request. If your child then states the "need" a pony, fifty meals a day, and an Apache helicopter in order to be happy, you may quickly become aware that your child is misguided. He or she can beg fervently for an Apache helicopter, but it isn't a sound request to make and an even worse request to answer. For what do you pray? Are you asking for ponies and Apaches? Keep in mind, G will not answer prayers that contradict Scripture. G is good. G is love. Prayers need to align with this understanding.

Let me tell you a story. Two men were shipwrecked on an island. The first man had little faith. The second man had great faith. Despite their differing opinions, they were good friends. Given their perilous fate and the little control they had over their circumstances, they agreed that the only thing left for them to do was to pray to G. The faithless man did not expect results from prayer, but he saw so no harm in the exercise. They thought it would be best to live on opposite sides of the island to ensure they didn't quickly grow tired of one another and because it would be interesting to see which man's prayers were answered.

The first night, the prayer was for food. The first man was pleased when he found a fruit-bearing tree with ripe, delicious fruit on his side of the island. The second man's side of the island remained barren.

The second prayer was for shelter. The next day, the first man discovered a storm had cleared the brush and revealed the opening of a cave that was warm and dry. The second man had nothing.

After some time had passed, the first man decided he was lonely and prayed for a wife. Miraculously enough, there was a shipwreck in the vicinity. The sole survivor was a woman who swam to the first man's side of the island. The first man prayed for clothing, more food, and entertainment. Everything he prayed for miraculously appeared.

One day, the first man prayed for him and his wife to be rescued. The next day, a ship was docked on the first man's side of the island. The man decided to leave the second man behind. He thought the other man was unworthy to partake of the blessings because none of the second man's prayers were answered. As the ship prepared to leave the harbor, G's voice surprised the first man. G asked "Why would you leave your dear companion on the island?"

The first man replied that the blessings were his alone since he was the one who asked for them. "My friend does not deserve anything because his prayers were not answered."

To this G replied, "To the contrary, he had only one prayer which I, indeed, did answer. If not for his prayer, you would have received nothing."

The first man said, "Tell me, for what did he pray that I should owe him anything?"

"He prayed that your prayers would be answered."

Actions and thoughts under Scripture and Prayer are the two steps that will allow you to gain wisdom. Wisdom does not mean leaning on your own understanding. That fallacy can be easily demonstrated by looking at how many people think some crazy things are right. Wisdom rests in the objective standard provided by the Creator in the written Word. Wisdom requires shifting thoughts from self to the bigger picture. These thoughts must be noble, trustworthy, kind. You humans carry your brains around with you wherever you go; you would think you would be more careful about what you put in them.

This is where Adam and Eve fell short. They both consciously and purposely chose to learn something bad. Adam actually broke G's directive, and Eve constructively broke the directive. Had they been strong in prayer, they would have had the wisdom to see the harm their choices would cause.

All people have the ability to control their minds and bodies in order to choose consciously from which tree they want to eat. If humans simply want to continue being their own self-created gods, containing all the power afforded a mere mortal, they have that right. You humans like to stand beside your self-created gods; but G stands beside the humans.

G is not divinity set up high in some distant world. G is integral to humanity, so much so that G was incarnated as a man—the Messiah. G knew that just providing the instructions à la Scripture would be insufficient for humans. As ordained at the time of creation, humans needed a prototype—a picture—of the Word lived out and a redeemer for the sins they would commit. This is Christ. Christ lived out the rules not by focusing on his physical actions but by training the heart. Once you learn to love, you can't help but act on this love. Jesus used all his strength to control his heart, soul, and mind.

Humans should spend their lives running to the Tree of Life. To run fast and well, you must drop your burdens, sins, and baggage.[218] You also must train your body and mind much like someone preparing for a marathon. G states, "To the one who is victorious, I will give the right to eat from the Tree of Life, which is in the paradise of G."

---

[218] Run naked. See Hebrews 11 and 12.

Act 7: Story Sabbath

I have been giving you all this background about Adam and Eve because so many humans think Scripture is simply a collection of short stories—like Aesop fables only less clear. Hopefully, when you read Scripture, the morals, prophesies, and deeper meanings that underlie each passage will resonate. Maybe if you read a passage, you will pause and think, *I wonder why that is in here.* I'm not dictating to you what G has said; rather, I am inviting you to explore G's Word more thoroughly. There is no limit to the depth of the Word.

I don't expect you to defer to me as the final authority, or I would start to emulate Adam. If you took my words at face value and do nothing else to relate with G, you would by default relate to Eve. Remember: her crime wasn't directly disobeying G; it was failing to find out what was expected of her. I would expect—well, hope—that you would explore Scripture and prayer on your own.

Ladies and gentlemen of the jury, Eve did not commit a worse offense than Adam, nor did she cause Adam to sin. She committed a different sin, and each human remains totally responsible and accountable for their own thoughts and actions. Humans cannot point to Eve or Adam and accuse them of anything they haven't done themselves.

I implore you to not look back in time to point to their sins and assess blame, but to look at your sins committed in the present. It is all about where you are going, not where you have been. This is not to say that history should be ignored but that historical acts do not provide justification for present sin.

When passing judgment, I humbly ask that you analyze whether your own thoughts and actions are focused on yourself or advancing the Kingdom of G. Now, much like a devout believer on the Sabbath, Defense rests.

www.ingramcontent.com/pod-product-compliance
Lightning Source LLC
Chambersburg PA
CBHW020415080526
44584CB00014B/1336